Highly Intuitive People

Highly Intuitive People

7 Right-Brain Traits to Change the Lives of Intuitive-Sensitive People

HEIDI SAWYER

HAY HOUSE

Carlsbad, California • New York City • London • Sydney
Johannesburg • Vancouver • Hong Kong • New Delhi

First published and distributed in the United Kingdom by:
Hay House UK Ltd, Astley House, 33 Notting Hill Gate, London W11 3JQ
Tel: +44 (0)20 3675 2450; Fax: +44 (0)20 3675 2451; www.hayhouse.co.uk

Published and distributed in the United States of America by:
Hay House Inc., PO Box 5100, Carlsbad, CA 92018-5100
Tel: (1) 760 431 7695 or (800) 654 5126; Fax: (1) 760 431 6948 or (800) 650 5115
www.hayhouse.com

Published and distributed in Australia by:
Hay House Australia Ltd, 18/36 Ralph St, Alexandria NSW 2015
Tel: (61) 2 9669 4299; Fax: (61) 2 9669 4144; www.hayhouse.com.au

Published and distributed in the Republic of South Africa by:
Hay House SA (Pty) Ltd, PO Box 990, Witkoppen 2068
Tel/Fax: (27) 11 467 8904; www.hayhouse.co.za

Published and distributed in India by:
Hay House Publishers India, Muskaan Complex, Plot No.3, B-2,
Vasant Kunj, New Delhi 110 070
Tel: (91) 11 4176 1620; Fax: (91) 11 4176 1630; www.hayhouse.co.in

Distributed in Canada by:
Raincoast Books, 2440 Viking Way, Richmond, B.C. V6V 1N2
Tel: (1) 604 448 7100; *Fax:* (1) 604 270 7161; www.raincoast.com

Text © Heidi Sawyer, 2015

The moral right of the author has been asserted.

The information given in this book should not be treated as a substitute for professional medical advice; always consult a medical practitioner. Any use of information in this book is at the reader's discretion and risk. Neither the author nor the publisher can be held responsible for any loss, claim or damage arising out of the use, or misuse, of the suggestions made, the failure to take medical advice or for any material on third party websites.

A catalogue record for this book is available from the British Library.

ISBN: 978-1-78180-476-6

Interior images: shutterstock.com

Printed and bound in Great Britain by TJ International Ltd, Padstow, Cornwall

Contents

Introduction

I've been working with Highly Intuitive People for more than 17 years, and I've discovered that other people have a radar for them. They seek their knowledge, beliefs and insight into all aspects of their lives – from relationships to career paths. For the Highly Intuitive Person though, this feels like a thankless task. Unless they offer something that the person asking wants to hear, their insight is ignored, even though it turns out to be correct. When it all goes wrong, they are the ones who are there to pick up the pieces and then go through it all again.

No-one hears them, no-one is there for their world; they provide the comfort, the missing pieces and the listening ear, yet they do not feel it for themselves. This book is for those unheard intuitive people.

When I started out, I never asked for intuitive ability – I didn't understand or want it. Like many Intuitive-Sensitives I felt lost in a sea of aloneness, surrounded by people who didn't seem to understand. We're labelled as the wise ones – we're perceptive, caring, emotionally generous with other people – but have little understanding of ourselves. We panic at the prospect of conflict and withdraw at the moment of overwhelm. This book contains the information I would have liked when I began – the instant answers I spent years searching for.

Some parts of the book will resonate with you more than others, but overall it will give you the healing tools for the Intuitive-Sensitive Person: a voice for your unheard world.

In the course of my work, people ask me these questions:

'Why am I so sensitive, and how can I tone it down?'

'Why is it I feel other people's emotions as though they are my own?'

'Why and how do I seem to see events in people's lives before they occur?'

'How do I get rid of overwhelm?'

Throughout my life I've had the opportunity to experience many extremes. They have taught me the richness of human faith, given me character strengths I never knew existed, and taught me the power of the intuitive journey to restore a passion for life.

What follows is your guidebook as an Intuitive-Sensitive Person: soul-seeker extraordinaire. It'll give you the depth you've been searching for, the answers that have eluded you. It will help you heal, and provide the route map to connecting with your own kind.

The world is changing. We've seen more developments in the last 15 years than in the previous 100, because of huge advances in technology. Those changes are set to continue, and as a species we're having to adapt faster than evolution allows. But no matter what technology demands of us tomorrow and no matter how advanced it becomes, it will never be able to truly understand human empathy.

The change has already begun – it's happening now. Around the world, senior people in organizations are seeking employees with a unique skill: one that can't be outsourced to countries with a cheaper labour force or automated. It's a skill that's natural to all Intuitive-Sensitives, and one that will be in huge demand, much sooner than any of us can predict. If you've ever voiced your concerns at work but had them dismissed, only to find that time proved you right and on the next occasion all heads turned to you (even though you may not be in a position of 'authority'), then this is set to continue.

True authority isn't handed down by those in power – it's given by the collective to those who deserve it. Intuitive-Sensitives are the secret leaders, and in perhaps only a few years from now, they will no longer be hidden, or silent.

Being thrust into the 'limelight' will be overwhelming, so I've written this book to help prepare you for this new demand on your nervous system. You can thrive in this new world. If I can do it, then so can you.

Part I

Understanding Yourself as an Intuitive-Sensitive Person

Part 1

Understanding Yourself
as an Intuitive-
Sensitive Person

Chapter 1

The Surgeon's Prayer

'And most important, have the courage to follow your heart and intuition. They somehow already know what you truly want to become; everything else is secondary.'
STEVE JOBS

'Back off, leave her alone – she's had enough.' Finally, someone had noticed I was finding the whole process more than a little overwhelming. Childbirth is the end of one's personal dignity at the best of times, but in my experience as an extreme Sensitive, it had become the choice point between life and death.

I lay clutching the side of the hospital trolley, trying not to cry. I was surrounded by 16 people – it's amazing how you can still manage to count when you're stressed – with what felt like fence post wires poking out of my femoral arteries. I looked around for the surgeon – a very nice woman whom I'd met numerous times in the build-up to this situation – hoping for some reassurance. She was standing in the corner with her hands covering her face, and she was moving into something much like the prayer position.

It was at that point that I had a blast of realization – the reason the surgeon wouldn't look me in the eye was nothing to do with whether she liked me or not, it was because she didn't want to be haunted for years to come by the eyes of the mother she couldn't be sure of saving.

I lay back onto the trolley, my white-knuckled hands letting go of the sides, and said nothing. As I looked up at the ceiling more and more excited faces appeared above me, all introducing themselves. Apparently what I was about to go through was a once-in-a-lifetime, not-to-be-missed learning opportunity for any obstetric medicine intern.

> In that moment of faith I had the most incredible experience of feeling. I had zero options — no choices at all. I knew that, if it came to the crunch, the surgeon would save the baby and let me go. She was aware that I had another son, and a husband, but there was only one option.

I can still hear myself saying the words 'What will be, will be' as I relaxed into feeling. I let the anaesthetist begin his job of injecting the drugs as I quietly mumbled the countdown to blackness.

Faith, trust, feeling and letting go

The true essence and power of 'letting go' is spoken of in many spiritual contexts – from experiencing or allowing 'God', to feeling completely at one with ourselves. We're all in search of some form of peace. For the sensitive person this is very obvious, and for the purely linear thinker, it's a subtle or distant thought only present when something uncomfortable happens.

My experience on the surgeon's table taught me what it really means to *feel*. Most of us spend our lives doing the opposite: we do anything possible to avoid feeling. Even for Highly Sensitive individuals, feelings are distant while emotions are forever present. We over-experience the world of other people; we take on their emotions as though they are our own. But we don't – as I discovered as I awaited my fate – properly access how we actually feel.

In my work I speak to many troubled people. They experience trouble with work, with relationships, with their finances – I've met trouble in its many forms. In my experience, people repeat their patterns in life – no matter how they wish to change it – unless they tackle one fundamental area: their relationship with faith.

The dictionary definition of faith says it's a 'complete trust or confidence in someone or something, or a strong belief in God or the doctrines of a religion'. My understanding of faith, in the context of deep personal development, has little to do with any set doctrines or values, and everything to do with building an inner level of connection to what is a deep faith in the *self*. This is a faith built on the firm foundations of feeling, trust and letting go.

For the sensitive person, the building of feeling, trust and letting go, in order to experience self-faith, eventually becomes a necessity rather than a luxury. Without it, we continue to experience the world as overwhelming, emotionally painful and at times soul-destroying, as our sensitivity directs us to hide, reject and yet at the same time desire deep, meaningful connection.

Deep faith and intuitive download

As I returned from the blackness, I found myself gazing around what I soon recognized as the hospital's recovery room. A nurse sprang to life when she realized I was returning to the world. It's funny what you observe during moments of deep stress: I remember the anaesthetist's kindness as he gently squeezed my hand to reassure me that I'd returned to the physical world; I remember his joke; and then I remember the pain. It's true what they say – tremendous pain does make it impossible to speak.

I'd just gone through surgery for a complete placenta previa and placenta accreta. Individually these are severe pregnancy complications, but together they could have resulted in my death. My body had held on for as long as it could, with my immune system under severe pressure from other complications, and it had been time to remove my son from the womb.

I'd known since the second scan that there was an issue; in fact I'd known for seven years. People ask me why there's a seven-year gap between my two children. This is the reason. It took me that long to build up the courage to do it again.

So how did I know I'd have the most severe complication they see in obstetric medicine? I knew because the intuitive self told me. It told me at the birth of my first son, when my blood pressure crashed and my face turned lily white, my lips blue. It told me his birth would complicate that of my second child. It said: 'You'll have to be careful with the next one; one false move and it'll kill you.' And sure enough, that's exactly what happened.

I was told to prepare myself for the worst, to put my affairs in order before the operation; to expect intensive care for weeks, if I survived. My blood was matched, prepared and ready, along with the forms to sign my womb away. The obstetrician, pen in hand and form under my nose, said: 'If you ever get pregnant again Heidi, it will kill you. We won't be able to save you.' Familiar words.

Some would say, with such clear insight, why would you have another child? Well, I had a very strong intuition that my second son was to come into the world. I can't put it into words, other than to say it was a deep intuition – one that wouldn't leave me alone. I finally plucked up the courage just before it was getting too late in life.

> Throughout the process a very deep intuition followed that I would be okay. It was a strong feeling of faith – a knowing that all was well. It seems that an intense state of long-term stress brings a serene awareness: perhaps a deeper connection to a different part of ourselves.

I didn't have the tunnel of light or an out-of-body experience – just a deep internal knowing that worry is futile. This went on for months. Indeed it largely remains with me now. A few days after the surgery, the surgeon sat on the end of my bed in the hospital. She said quietly: 'Some kind of miracle happened in there, Heidi. So much so, that I can't believe it. I'm sorry, but I had to open you up again to check.'

She told me she'd had some kind of powerful experience – of serenity and calmness – as she'd made the incision for the surgery. She explained how the room and everyone in it had become incredibly peaceful: it was like nothing she'd known in her 30-year career. But she couldn't help adding that my situation had put 20 years on her!

Miraculously, even though she'd made sure it was now useless, the surgeon had managed to save my womb. I was grateful, as I wasn't yet ready to give it up. I did do so a year later, along with my ovaries, but I needed the time – as any woman does, perhaps – to think about going through that particular surgery at a young age. It was the time I needed to grieve the letting go of what I believed was my womanhood.

The whole process taught me that intuition is a deep faith and trust in our inner world. I learned that day to appreciate that the over-working and over-pleasing part of the intuitive nature doesn't have to stay that way: it can settle into perspective. With continual inner training, Intuitive-Sensitivity can be a *blessing* rather than a painful part of our deepest nature, something we should try to eliminate in order to make us 'normal'. Without it, I wouldn't be alive today.

That day, Halloween 2011, brought into the world a lovely little boy, for whom I'm deeply grateful. He's a gentle soul with, of course, a sensitive nature.

Chapter 2

What is an Intuitive-Sensitive Person?

'Beauty of whatever kind, in its supreme development,
invariably excites the sensitive soul to tears.'
EDGAR ALLAN POE

The term 'Highly Sensitive People' was coined by Dr Elaine Aron, an American clinical and research scientist, and it refers to a personality trait found in a section of society – an estimated 15–20 per cent of the population.[1] The basis of Dr Aron's theory – which has attracted quite extensive scientific research in recent years – is that Highly Sensitive People have a nervous system that's more aware of life's subtleties because their brains process and reflect information more deeply.[2]

Biologists have found that this Highly Sensitive trait exists in at least 100 species, and it's considered a survival strategy. The Highly Sensitive animal or human is *extra aware*: it can see more vividly than others do, but at the same time it's easily overwhelmed.[3] If we look at this in terms of a herd of animals, we'll see a portion who are extra observant – they *feel* where the best land is and where the sources of water are located, and generally know when it's time to move on. That skill is subtle – it's directive yet cautious.

The rest of the herd will find themselves following the actions of these sensitive protectors, who are observant enough to know when to move and when to keep still. In humans this Highly Sensitive trait has been largely overlooked and sidelined, and as a result, the people who possess it feel there's something wrong with them – and their sensitivity impacts their self-esteem.

Intuitive-Sensitivity: a form of High Sensitivity

After 17 years of interacting with thousands of people who defined themselves as both Highly Sensitive and Intuitive-Sensitive, I've come to realize that while all Intuitive-Sensitive People are Sensitives, not all Sensitives are Intuitive.

An Intuitive-Sensitive Person shows as a refined, exaggerated type of Highly Sensitive Person. My view of Intuitive-Sensitivity comes from working with people who describe themselves as deeply intuitive – something they often find confusing and somewhat worrying. They're concerned about what others might – or already do – think of their apparently finely tuned instincts: their ability to see situations for what they are, rather than what the world would like to see them as, as well as their inherent sensitivity.

> Intuitive-Sensitive People tend to be the Highly Sensitive individuals who want to explore their sensitivity for the good of themselves and others. They want to know what their intuition is about, how to use it properly and why they have it.

In my experience, Intuitive-Sensitivity seems to come from an issue linked to nurturance in our early lives, which is either consciously part of our world, or a part of our unconscious heritage – we'll be looking at this in depth, later in the book.

Intuitive-Sensitives have, in the majority of cases, developed an additional component to their sensitivity as a layer of emotional self-protection. This 'extra' part is an extra-sensory skill over and above the normal senses.

I've also discovered that Intuitive-Sensitivity is a *hidden* trait, one that Intuitive-Sensitives keep quiet from their outer world. Numerous professional people have confessed to me their extra-sensory skills: I've had doctors, barristers, CEOs, even a university law professor tell me about their secret psychic world. But Intuitive-Sensitivity impacts or 'happens' to people from all walks of life: the homemaker, the accountant, the man who's afraid to tell his wife that he has extra-sensory experiences.

Extra-sensory skills and intuitive instincts

The one thing these people have in common though, is that their skills and instincts were not asked for – they just appeared. They often began early in childhood, before promptly disappearing for a big chunk of the person's life and then returning around the same time that other types of sensory overload became apparent. Intuitive-Sensitive skills show in several formats. They usually follow a process, but generally the following aspects are present:

Premonitions

Firstly, there's a general feeling of seeing or knowing things before they occur. For some this feeling is extremely obvious and psychic in nature: they see these things in their sleep state, and they have a relaxed insight into people's lives – an ability to see outcomes beyond 'You'll meet a tall, dark, handsome stranger' and predicting lottery numbers.

It's more to do with an insight into other people and how they feel. This will often relate to relationships, work scenarios and anything to do with danger. The insight often occurs in a spontaneous manner – many Intuitive-Sensitives have very vivid experiences of feeling another's energy, their life situation and the outcome to what may be creating upset. Sometimes this insight isn't popular with their nearest and dearest, who see it as 'doom thinking' or meddling. Therefore I see quite a few upset Intuitive-Sensitives who can't get through to the people they love.

In the early days, Intuitive-Sensitives find this inability to get through very distressing because they feel it's their job to help solve or rescue. This sensitivity to seeing things in their dream or waking state before they manifest in reality, causes many a moral dilemma; they ask themselves: 'Should I or shouldn't I speak up?'

Often, it's a thankless task, mentioning things that someone hasn't asked for, and this starts to impact the Intuitive-Sensitives self-esteem. Their insights are often ignored or discounted, but then they discover, months later, that what they predicted has in fact happened. But *how* did they know it? Is it some kind of magical ability? Is it really possible to predict an outcome when you have little to no information?

Many theorize that intuitive instincts beyond the norms of human behaviour are a fallacy of the deluded. This belief upsets and confuses the true Intuitive-Sensitive because their deepest nature, something they can't help or stop themselves from being part of, is marginalized and made unacceptable.

They go on to question whether their perceptive instincts are indeed the result of an over-productive imagination or even a serious mental health issue. I always reassure those who question their sanity that insane people don't notice they're not quite right. They tend to believe there's nothing wrong with them – it's everyone else.

The Intuitive-Sensitive, however, believes that everyone else is right and there's something wrong with *them*. As they're very sensitive to energy, they see things before they occur, are very perceptive when it comes to other people, don't suffer fools, are hyper-vigilant and can't be bothered with polite conversations about the weather – they want to get to the juicy stuff or not bother at all.

> Intuitive-Sensitives take two seconds flat to decide if they like or dislike someone. That decision isn't based on looks, how someone appears, or the persona they present, it's placed on what they 'feel'. All of which does appear, on the surface, to put them in the land of la-la – hence the reason they sometimes question their sanity.

This is especially difficult because our social programming has trained us to be polite, to put others first and never to express how we really feel. This builds an enormous pressure in the Intuitive-Sensitive, especially as most have a paralyzing fear of confrontation. This isn't usually because they're scared or nervous people – although as it affects people from all walks of life, some are – it's because confrontation actually physically *hurts* them.

They have to deal with their own sensory information around the confrontation and also process the emotions of the *other* person. If that emotion is anger, it'll cut into something deep in their stomach region, way beyond 'butterflies'. If it's hurt, then they feel enormous guilt for bringing it up and upsetting the other person. For the Intuitive-Sensitive, confrontation is about bracing yourself, preparing for the energetic onslaught.

Sensory overload

In seminar presentations, when I explain why an Intuitive-Sensitive Person will do a 'perfume dash' through a department store, or why, when visiting a restaurant, they'd rather leave than have to sit at a table with their back to the door, or how, at a dinner party they'll hang around to make sure they get the end seat on a rectangular table, but don't mind where they sit on a round table, there's always a deep chuckle of recognition.

But why do they do these things? The answer is: information overload. To an Intuitive-Sensitive the perfume counter smells like a chemical factory, designed to give them a headache. When people dine out in a restaurant they expect to be able to relax and enjoy their meal, but for the Intuitive-Sensitive who finds themselves seated with their back to the door, it's anything but relaxing. The diners coming into the restaurant have questions in their minds: where will they sit? Where are the friends they're due to meet? And then there are the nervous ones on a first date....

All this information is picked up by the Intuitive-Sensitive's awareness, although they haven't even *seen* these people. It makes them feel vulnerable, exposed to others' emotions when they don't want to be. They want to eat in peace. They aren't aware of this in the early days – then all they know is that their general feelings switch every few minutes while they're eating. When they can seat themselves *facing* the door, though, it seems they're more in control of how they feel – not so caught unawares.

And why the rectangular table? Intuitive-Sensitives discover that the people in a group who like to be in control, or who are particularly nervous, will head towards a central seat. Those people will be worrying about what they'll order and how the bill will be split, and the Intuitive-Sensitive doesn't want to be processing all of that. They've gone out to interact with their friends, not to be in the unconscious firing line of a stranger's mind.

They feel so much better sitting at the end of the table, with just one person on one side whose energy they have to deal with and, usually, the other sensitive person opposite them. They have plenty to discuss with these people, beyond the weather and polite chitchat. The conversation turns to deeper matters in a short space of time, while the socially anxious are desperate to clamber to the central seats, to have competitive conversations with plenty of nervous laughter. They avoid the 'deep' people at the end, whom they often initially mistake as shy.

Intuitive-Sensitivity and wisdom

Strongly perceptive wisdom is a part of the Intuitive-Sensitive's make-up, and it's often been present since their early years. Often mistaken as shy in childhood, the Intuitive-Sensitive Person was busy working out how others view the world, and it wasn't long before they realized others don't seem to share their values.

For some, this led to a feeling of emotional isolation, as their overly responsible nature sought to look after others before they were mature enough to do so. Many were called 'mini adults' or 'wise babies', but without the precocious attitude. Theirs is a quiet, subtle level of natural wisdom. Later in life, as the Intuitive-Sensitive tries to shrug off this wisdom, they often have to make compromised decisions in order to fit in. This is part of their tendency to want to 'save' others; to avoid like the plague any kind of judgement; and to feel safe and loved.

This compromised self survives into adulthood, especially if they've come from a background that taught them to value what others think over and above their own perceptions. It's not until the shame, guilt and sense of duty is really *felt* that the intuitive sense starts to really knock on their inner door.

The question is, why do Intuitive-Sensitives suddenly become aware of their deeper senses? I believe the brain triggers this awareness as a strong survival instinct, so the already Intuitive-Sensitive Person who has stepped up a gear once too often can protect themselves from an emotional breakdown when their overwhelmed senses become too much to bear. The 'switch' happens when the Intuitive-Sensitive has had enough of feeling pushed from pillar to post. It's an unconscious trigger that gradually becomes conscious.

Stress and the Intuitive-Sensitive

Stress is a normal, everyday occurrence for an Intuitive-Sensitive, just as it is for most people. The difference is that many Intuitive-Sensitives are great in a crisis – they're the ones who don't panic, the ones who seem to know almost instantly what to do. Their nervous system doesn't shut down when difficulty strikes – in fact, it comes to life. To them, this kind of external stress is almost a pleasurable relief from the internal stress they live with constantly.

There are many aspects of the Highly Sensitive Person that cross into the Intuitive-Sensitive Person. The Intuitive-Sensitive swims in the pool of life like everyone else, but while others respond with a gentle breaststroke in warm, sometimes cool waters, they find themselves flapping at a manic pace with all kinds of stuff wrapped around their feet. Sometimes it's seaweed, sometimes it's an unusual fish trying to nibble their feet; at other times they see the shark coming while everyone else is oblivious or slow to react.

The trouble is that Intuitive-Sensitives have a vivid mind. Every one I've ever met had a very alert, elaborate memory. They remember fine detail, usually associated with emotional impact. On the one hand this is incredibly useful, but on the other it means they don't forget. Their entire nervous system is run by ongoing memory. It pipes up, *Don't put your foot there. Remember the last time you did that? We got covered in seaweed for weeks. Oh, and remember that shift in the feel of things… before the shark came? Watch what you do there, and dodge the spot where it was icy cold last time.*

This kind of ongoing internal pressure would turn most people into a neurotic mess. The Intuitive-Sensitive, however, has learned how to negotiate their internal minefield, so it often appears completely 'handled' in their external world. That's not to say they put on a performance; in fact, it's usually the complete opposite – they need honesty. Why? Well, it's tough enough looking out for everything in the pool of life without having to deal with others' denial and panic over the seaweed they've never experienced before.

A lack of honesty is what really creates a deep stress in the Intuitive-Sensitive. This is because their empathetic nature feels highly responsible for the emotions others cannot access. Their refined senses mean they're constantly interpreting energy – they just can't help it. They walk into a situation and live out the energy of it – they feel it in work environments, within a room, even in a new house purchase.

Yet although they experience a continuous sensory overload, Intuitive-Sensitives aren't emotional heaps who are unable to function in life. They are made of tough stuff – they get up, dust themselves down and carry on. They can do this because of the development of faith.

This faith appears through an internal instinct rather than being triggered by an external event or interest. I believe it's an emotional survival drive for the Intuitive-Sensitive to feel they want to develop their intuitive instincts – to help them successfully weave through the fires of life, with only the occasional burn. It may have taken a while for them to become aware they have these intuitive skills, as they regard them as normal and believe that everyone has them. Their interest returns to them later in life, despite the fact they tried to abandon it in childhood.

The feeling of 'going home'

Every Intuitive-Sensitive I've come across has had a feeling inside of 'wanting to go home'. When I've discussed this observation with an audience, tears stream down people's faces, they fidget and they look around. They're not quite sure what to do with themselves. The reason for this is that they thought this sense of 'wanting to go home' was something quiet, a feeling no-one else acknowledged; they believed it was only them who felt it.

For Intuitive-Sensitives, home doesn't have a name. It isn't a place they understand – it's not a house or a location to move to. It's a feeling they recognize somewhere deep inside. They've had some kind of experience that has given them a glimpse of this feeling, and it's one they are keen to return to.

To an Intuitive-Sensitive, the feeling of 'home' is a strong motivator in life. In fact, I'd say it's their main focus. They want and are willing to create the feeling in their life experience; they want to live rather than to exist. Their sensory perceptions, their intuition-based focus, is something they want to use positively in the physical world. Their desire for meaning, purpose and acceptance is strong enough to drive them to make a real difference, even if they're scared.

They need and want though, to let go of worrying about what others think – they need to figure out how to manage risk and neutralize their own misjudgements or wishful thinking. The feeling of 'home' offers this safety from the fear of criticism and a release from the pressure of perfection, although it's their perfectionist nature that contributes to their empathetic gentleness.

In a world where logic is valued more highly than emotion, the feeling of 'home', however briefly felt at some point in an Intuitive-Sensitive's life, has a strong foundation in their intuitive nature. The word 'intuition' comes from a Latin verb meaning 'to look inside': to internalize contemplation. To the Intuitive-Sensitive, the experience of returning 'home' is a feeling where the world of the personality (logic) collides with the world of emotion.

The true self

Intuition generally provides views or judgements that cannot be empirically verified, and this makes 'proving' intuitional processes very difficult, especially here in the West, where 'logic is king'. The Intuitive-Sensitive Person worries whether their intuitive self is true, rather than just a figment of their over-productive imagination, and most importantly, they are concerned that it's not the basis of making them somehow 'fake'. This internalized pressure creates an emotional division between the logical self and the basis of the 'soul's process', which is based on an honesty of emotion: a component of what's often referred to as the 'true self'.

So what is the 'true self'? Has anyone ever seen this elusive creature? Are we not simply made up of our brain's function and isn't the true self some fluffy, made-up concept? There's plenty of very convincing evidence to suggest that the former is true. However, I believe, even if we're simply our brain, the intelligence that tells us how to proceed, how to make the brain work, must and does come from a universal intelligence.

That universal intelligence is based in intuition – it's the link to the unconfined, the untrainable: the level of energy that has a mind and intelligence of its own. It won't be controlled or manipulated. The true self therefore is free flowing – it has a mind of its own and it enjoys its freedom. We experience ourselves as the true self the moment we let go of trying to control outcomes. What the Intuitive-Sensitive wants in life is to find a level of self-acceptance.

Chapter 3

'You're Too Sensitive'

'You go through spells where you feel that maybe you're too sensitive for this world. I certainly felt that.'
WINONA RYDER

Andrea arrived home from work, kicked off her shoes and headed straight for the fridge. She opened the door and looked longingly inside for the remains of the chocolate bar she'd carefully hidden in the fridge door the previous night. She'd had a bad day – a colleague had joked about the quality of her work because she'd made a minor mistake. She never made mistakes, and her colleague had been quick to point this one out. She was sure he hadn't meant any harm, but even so, the comment had hurt her.

Andrea peeled off what was left of the wrapper, and breaking one of the last four squares with her teeth, sloshed the silky smooth chocolate around her mouth. Instantly she felt calm. She then switched on the TV and sat quietly, mindlessly gazing at the screen as she enjoyed her few moments of peace before anyone else came home.

Intuitive–Sensitive People strongly question things – they question the meaning of life, right down to where they fit *in, and this is something they've experienced for a very long time. They can't cope with the mundane — it's painful for them, and they want to be part of something with meaning. More importantly, they want deep connection.*

When others joke about them or criticize them, the energy of such things cuts a very deep wound. They may take it lightly on the surface, but underneath, they're plotting to leave that situation as quickly as they possibly can. I'm sure most people have a sensitivity to criticism; after all, we want be liked and we don't like to offend others – we prefer to keep the peace. In this way, many events in life are overlooked and ignored: people just don't want to get involved.

But the Intuitive-Sensitive is caught in a world where criticism is a distinct fear. They will go to great lengths to avoid it, unless the situation involves someone who means a lot to them, in which case they'll defend themselves to the hilt, but always try hard to make sure their response is fair and just. The way that they deal with criticism keeps them awake at night. Should they or shouldn't they do it? How do they approach it? What will be the consequences?

The chocolate-criticism connection

For the Intuitive-Sensitive, criticism brings up such a feeling of deep anxiety it not only impacts their feelings, it also impacts how they interact with food. In my experience, those individuals who've had a particularly powerful early life experience around criticism – an overly critical parent, for example – will be strongly attracted to chocolate.

Why chocolate? Serotonin, the happy brain chemical that lowers the stress response, has long been a partner with chocolate. On occasion, I've experimented with groups of intuitive people during workshops, dividing them into groups according to their favourite sugar item – for some it's cakes, others biscuits, and of course, for many it's chocolate.

I've found that certain emotions are a strong match in these groups. For the chocolate people, it's criticism. They eat chocolate in a secretive manner; they try to make sure that people (even themselves) don't notice how much of it they eat. The group, when presented with copious amounts of chocolate and the permission to eat it, politely refuse. Some break off four squares, nibble them, then neatly fold the top and go no further. The others won't even touch the chocolate, claiming they don't want or need it.

In public, their emotions wouldn't allow them to eat chocolate or even to acknowledge that they wanted it. Their story was very different when I then took the chocolate away, putting it straight into a waste sack. Then they were scrabbling to try to save it, angry that it was going to waste. It was at this point that their true emotions emerged.

They were secretive because they feared criticism for eating the chocolate, yet a strong anger and enraged rebellion made them want to eat it in private. When I asked these people about their behaviour afterwards, each one said that they had indeed had at least one highly critical parent.

This isn't to say that all chocoholics have a critical parent. However, every Intuitive-Sensitive Person I've met whose favourite source of sugar is chocolate has experienced this, and there's too much evidence, from thousands of people, to dismiss this. These individuals' Highly Intuitive instincts have emerged as some form of defence or protection mechanism. It's become an ability to protect and ward-off criticism by being able to accurately pre-judge or even accurately pre-see situations.

Attachment and an inherited fear of criticism

Humiliation, worrying about what others think and displays of anger or shouting are areas of deep concern for the Intuitive-Sensitive Person working out their level of sensitivity. It also impacts in terms of their deepest fear: humiliation. These things hold back the Intuitive-Sensitive in all areas of their life. They prevent them from speaking up, engaging in certain activities or voicing their irritation before the point of outrage.

As we learned in the last chapter, there's a strong indication that natural sensitivity is a trait you're born with.[1] It isn't dependent on being intuitive, although Sensitives do notice more; in fact, some would say 'noticing more' is the only basis of intuitive instinct. But I believe Intuitive-Sensitives have something deeper. This depth, the link to spiritual matters – for some it's the link to God, to others it's to spiritual experiences, healing, psychic insight, interpreting energy or Buddhist principles – comes from a subconscious need to experience a deeper connection to love.

Attachment theory is a psychological theory that has gained enormous ground over the last few decades. Originating from the work of psychoanalyst John Bowlby, it's centred on the emotional bonds between people, and it suggests that the earliest of these bonds, or lack of them, can leave a lasting impression on our lives. It says that humans need to form a deep relationship with their primary caregiver in early life for successful social and emotional development to take place. This relationship, or bond, is also believed to be crucial for our ability to self-regulate our feelings.

Personally, I've noticed a big change in how this area is approached around childbirth. When my eldest son was born in 2004, the maternity department strongly encouraged us new mothers to make skin-to-skin contact as soon as it was safely possible, even after as complicated a delivery as mine had been. By 2011, when my youngest was born, the skin-to-skin contact was obligatory, even though on that occasion I was barely functioning!

The reason given was the need to build the baby's immune system, but really attachment is a lot more than that. Anyone born in many parts of the Western world during the 1960s, 70s, and perhaps part of the 80s, was separated from their mother and placed in a nursery shortly after birth. Having been safe and comfortable swimming around in the womb, life was suddenly sprung upon us.

We were separated from our original source of comfort: the scent of our mother; the sound of her voice; our familiar, albeit muffled, surroundings during our nine months in the womb. These all abruptly concluded with no contact with mum, set feeding times and the sound of other screaming babies.

During these decades, little thought was given to the baby and its developing brain, and as products of the 'children should be seen and not heard' era, those of us born in this era have quietly accepted this very early level of compromise.

Perhaps one of the reasons why so many children born today are more bold and forthcoming in their views and confidence is because they arrived during a time when immediate human contact after birth was encouraged, thus ensuring their nervous systems had a firmer foundation.

If we go back further, those born in Europe and elsewhere during the 1940s and 50s have the remnants of World War II as part of their psyche. And the generations before them were born into a time of deep stress: the horrors of World War I and its aftermath. In those eras infant attachment and early foundations were not top of the agenda.

This energy has filtered down through the generations: certainly in the UK we still have that wartime 'keep calm and carry on' mentality. This isn't helpful to the Intuitive-Sensitive individual, who feels the undertones of others' feelings as though they are their own, yet on the surface will deny their emotions as though their life depends on it. The denial of emotions lead to insecurity hidden as power, and when this happens, it comes out in another person as criticism.

Intuitive-Sensitive People who were heavily criticized by a parent (or parents) weren't able to brush off that criticism: it cut very deeply, more so than was intended. Also, if they didn't form a strong early bond with that parent, if the attachment wasn't deep enough, it left an emotional space – one that they later filled with the unconscious belief that *in order to be loved (attached) I must be criticized.* That belief can filter into their adult relationships – they'll always be waiting, with trepidation, to be criticized. If this doesn't show in their outer relationships it'll certainly show internally: with the self. They will become their own worst critic.

If an Intuitive-Sensitive *has* experienced a critical parent, it's often the case that the parent had a tough start in life themselves: there may have been attachment issues during their formative years – perhaps their parents abandoned them emotionally – and this may have led them to believe that their sensitive child needs to 'toughen up'. Perhaps presenting them with the 'cold, hard facts of life' – which they, too, had to face – will do the job?

For the Intuitive-Sensitive, then, along with criticism, emotional abandonment also becomes strongly associated with love. There's often an unconscious belief that they need to remain emotionally distant and be incredibly self-sufficient, even though they're sensitive, because at some point the people they become close to will leave them. There's a point in time when the Sensitive mind wants to evolve beyond defining the self as someone who deserves criticism. It appears that this unconscious desire triggers the unfolding of the intuitive process. The person begins to switch into seeing life through the eyes of intuition and a deeper connection with the self.

Why does this happen? Seemingly, it's the stage at which the psyche – the unconscious world of the person – wants to have a connection to unconditional love. This is a love that the person has never felt from another. It's a 'soul love' – something beyond words – but it's deeply connected. It somehow replaces the 'lost' love of insecure attachment.

This is often the beginning of switching from being Sensitive into becoming an Intuitive-Sensitive. For some, the connection to unconditional love begins with an attraction or belief in angels; for others it's an experience of psychic insight through dreams or feeling guided. Whatever the experience, the opening of intuitive insight and consciously working with it develops a sense of security and relief from what is for some, depressed feelings or anxiety.

This isn't to say that all Highly Intuitive People have experienced parental criticism or emotional abandonment – your own parents may have been ultra kind to compensate for what they lacked in their early life. However, it's likely that you've come from generations of them, or at the very least, from the era of infant emotional abandonment. The cool facts are that this poor early start has impacted generations going forwards, and it suggests why you were born so sensitive.

Intuitive-Sensitives and autoimmune disease

Recently I conducted a survey among a group of people who define themselves as Highly Intuitive to see if there was a possible connection between that and the incidence of autoimmune disease. (I did this mostly out of interest, because I wanted to see if the link was my imagination or a definable trait.) I enlisted the help of a medical doctor, and more than 2,000 Highly Intuitive People completed the survey. The results were analysed, and they showed a rate of autoimmune-related health issues 30 per cent higher than the UK national average. But the question is: why?

Clinical research shows that chronic stress can impair the body's immunity. Studies have shown that attachment insecurity – characterized by difficulty trusting others, worrying about being abandoned and feeling uncomfortable with emotional intimacy – can impact the 'killer' cells that defend our body against illness. This suggests that early attachment issues can impact adult attachment issues (how we relate/trust in romantic relationships, especially once we've been hurt) and can go on to impact our health.

Childhood trauma has been linked to a heightened risk of serious disease, including autoimmune disorders.[1] In some circumstances, people with autoimmune disease have an abnormal range of cortisol levels. Cortisol is a hormone made in the cortex of the adrenal glands, then released into the blood. Almost every cell in the body contains receptors for cortisol, including those that control the body's blood sugar levels and therefore the regulation of our metabolism. Cortisol acts as an anti-inflammatory; it influences our memory; and it controls our body's water and salt levels. In addition, it's responsible for the way the body deals with stress.

Many Intuitive-Sensitives, regardless of whether or not they have autoimmune issues, state that they have symptoms associated with stressed adrenal glands – the adrenals having become tired from the pressure of producing high levels of cortisol. They have a heavy interest in sugar, central abdominal fat (even if they're generally slim), intense fatigue and signs of inflammation. Many of these symptoms are also called stress! Given that in order to be intuitive you have a higher than average nervous system response to stimuli, stress will be your middle name.

> For some Intuitive-Sensitives, the extra pressure on their system may result in an autoimmune condition called Chronic Fatigue Syndrome. I've seen that for many of these people, the stress response of Chronic Fatigue is a part of their internal world – perhaps even the inner child calling out for nurturance.

At an unconscious level, the child self feels that the emotional world is too overwhelming for them to process. The resulting stress means the cortisol receptors in the body flood and stop working properly because this 'overwhelm' is too strong for them.

This process is a little like the conveyor belt at the end of a supermarket checkout. How frustrated we get if the person operating the till is in too much of a hurry to turn the belt off and give us a chance to pack our shopping before it gets crushed. With Chronic Fatigue, the cortisol receptors become so overwhelmed by the metaphorical conveyor belt, that everything gets squashed and stuck to the extent that it no longer works properly and the 'system' collapses.

The conveyor belt stops working altogether, and this shows in the body as what feels like a system failure. Nothing appears to work properly, and the tiredness becomes extreme. In an effort to protect itself, the body continues with its shut-down: the Chronic Fatigue appearing as something 'unexplained', often put down to an 'emotional' condition.

Cortisol neurones are grown in babyhood as a response to the mother's nurturing. The mother feels safe in the world, and as a result, so does the baby; this is achieved through the mother's feeding and touch.[2] The baby is protected from stress, and as a result, its brain grows more cortisol neurones. And more cortisol neurones means the body has a greater propensity to deal with the stress response.

Within the survey results I collected, there did appear to be a close connection between some aspects of autoimmune conditions, the way in which stress is processed in Intuitive-Sensitive People, and a gap in aspects of early development associated with nurturing. Many of those who took part in the survey said they'd had early life problems they'd learned to deal with. Some had had emotionally or physically unavailable parent(s), and others commented on how they were aware that, although their parents had been kind and loving, their grandparents had been unavailable to their own children.

Among the survey participants there was an unusually high incidence of rheumatoid arthritis, Hashimoto's disease (a thyroid condition) and chronic long-term autoimmune issues. There were also common reports of uncommon conditions. I've lost count of the number of Intuitive-Sensitives I've met who have been diagnosed with endocrine conditions, such as Addison's Disease and lesions on the pituitary gland.

The medical professional I explored the survey with was surprised by the unusually high incidence of autoimmune conditions in a single group of individuals. We concluded that the main area of consistency seemed to be around early life influences involving some form of emotional trauma. The Intuitive-Sensitives with no trauma in their backgrounds seemed to be the ones who were free of autoimmune issues.

Cortisol, stress and right-brain preference

The brain is split into two halves: the left and right hemispheres, also known as the left-brain and right-brain. It's a popular perception that the left-brain represents logical thinking, and the right creative thinking, although neuroscience has discovered that the whole brain is involved in our thinking, with neither hemisphere dominating. However, the 'left-brain/right-brain' idea remains an ideal way of describing a concept.

Neuroscience does agree though, that the right hemisphere has more connections to the nervous system. There's an argument that those who are sensitive to their environment – hyper-vigilant, intuitive and therefore sensitive – have a right-brain preference that is thought to be the basis of heightened sensitivity. This means that in order for a person to be a Sensitive, there has to have been some form of stress within the womb to create a right-brain preference.

In addition, high cortisol levels are associated with a highly active right-brain and a less active left-brain.[3] This would possibly account for the fact that Highly Intuitive People often have elevated cortisol levels: they have more connectors to the nervous system and thus a higher propensity to create cortisol.

The majority of people have a more active left- than right-brain.[4] This would potentially make them calmer, and less susceptible to stressors. They would therefore be linked more to what would be termed an extroverted outlook, and be less aware or impacted by environments.

Sensitive and certainly Highly Intuitive People are likely to have a more active right-brain, making them more 'jumpy' in their environment. Their sensitivity makes them take what some would see as a 'joke' as personal criticism.

In many instances jokes are indeed that – they're a criticism or a way to devalue a person, but those who have a more active left-brain are better able to shrug it off.

If the Highly Intuitive Person has continually experienced stress throughout their life – whether due to their natural predisposition to it or as a result of a stressful early life – their cortisol levels will be higher than normal. Susan Gerhardt, a pioneering psychotherapist in child observation, suggests that a child who's continually devalued and criticized will accept a lower social status within the family in order to survive.

This may well explain why many Highly Intuitive People have to work at healing their desire to people-please, rather than properly accessing their own needs. Even though a Highly Intuitive Person has an apparent challenge over and above the norm around criticism, early nurturing and the management of stress, I've seen how many have the ability to heal, *over and above* the norm. They are incredibly easy people to work with –

their intuitive skills allow them an easily balanced access to their internal world, with a strong willingness to change.

Over the years I've seen Highly Intuitive People make their way positively, despite some extraordinary levels of emotional abandonment. Different to others who have experienced abusive foundations, they do their best to bounce through it, healing the unpleasantness in their early background. Some have been on the receiving end of pathological narcissism, alcoholism in the family, emotional and sometimes physical violence, yet they seek their way to heal these experiences.

Why Intuitive-Sensitive People have a kind heart

In my experience, Intuitive-Sensitive People are as consciously unselfish as they can possibly be. They consistently seek to help others, and want to contribute in life and put their naturally caring skills to good use. They are highly perceptive, relate well to other people, and feel overly emotionally responsible for their wellbeing. Even when they've been through some form of physical hardship, they want to engage with something that might again put their body or emotions through overload.

But why would they do this? It's because they have a level of empathy that absorbs like a sponge. They feel completely emotionally responsible for their environment, including a need to fix anger for other people. They are extremely uneasy with anger – a person doesn't have to show anger outwardly for them to feel very uncomfortable.

Often this anger is either unconscious or semi-conscious for the person experiencing it, yet the Intuitive-Sensitive can feel the undertone. They can feel the energetic pressure in the person's mind and body. This, on occasion, will be expressed through the Intuitive: they'll suddenly have angry thoughts or feelings when previously they felt fine.

This happens in the company of other people, which is why an Intuitive-Sensitive will often feel completely exhausted when there's an unconscious anger happening in a situation. This isn't to say they are in any way emotionally awkward – often it's the opposite – but they are emotionally hugely connected and enjoy engagement with others. However, they'll come away totally drained if they have to lighten up a scenario by processing through their own emotions the unhappy thoughts of another.

In many situations the Intuitive-Sensitive Person will try their very best with people. They'll find solutions to problems when others have failed; they'll take care of a person's needs as if they were their own; and they'll sacrifice their own life as a selfless act for another.

Much of the time, though, these efforts go unrewarded. They ask for little from others, while pre-empting their needs. They start to develop an uncanny ability to predict what's needed next – to the point of intuiting others' lives or their healing requirements.

When they get to the point of feeling emotionally overwhelmed, though, they withdraw completely – into their own world, and away from others. This is the point at which every Sensitive individual needs recovery time. Their nervous system is now in overload, and they need to withdraw into the background in order to gather both their thoughts and their physical health. Without this withdrawal, the Intuitive-Sensitive will find that their health starts to become compromised.

This is the point at which, if they are of 'service' to an individual, especially a co-dependent one, the Intuitive-Sensitive will be on the receiving end of their anger. The other person will disapprove of their withdrawal, saying they are 'too sensitive', or they'll criticize whatever new interest they've found in order to cope with the overload. For many Intuitive-Sensitives, their new interest will be the development of their intuitive skills or healing.

This cycle puts the Intuitive-Sensitive in a difficult position. In order to avoid a system 'shut-down' they need to recover from the stimulation overload, yet they are faced with their biggest fear in another person – anger. They feel emotionally responsible for others and don't want an argument, yet feel they need to 'solve' anger in another person. And if they can't fix it, they will leave: they can only compromise themselves for so long before a survival mechanism directed towards self-preservation kicks in.

This is why many, before they become conscious of their sensitivity, go through relationships that are dogged by significant communication and boundary issues. Once the Intuitive-Sensitive feels they aren't the only one who experiences their emotional world through their hyper-sensitive senses, finding that they have a strong desire to discover their healing and intuitive interests, they develop the ability to relax. They do this because they have a new source of love, and this love is unconditional: it's not hard work and it doesn't involve other people and having to process their emotional world.

This new love is the beginning of the development of unconditional kindness, and the simplest form of this to find but the hardest to achieve is unconditional kindness *towards the self*. This is achieved through the natural intuitive opening that the

Intuitive-Sensitive begins to trigger in their life, mixed with a strong desire to heal.

Gina's story

When I first met Gina she was a timid, shy person. When she spoke I could hardly hear her because her voice was so quiet. She was keen to find out about her sensitivity, but she didn't want to be intrusive, so she asked almost apologetically. Deeper into our conversation I discovered that she'd been through Chronic Fatigue that had wiped her out for five years. She'd brought up two sons and now wanted to explore a role that would involve helping others.

When I looked into Gina's life I could see that if she followed this particular career path imminently she'd very quickly burn out. I told her that she had quite a lot to work through in her inner world before she could process the emotions of others without taking them on personally. I believed she had 'lost her voice' early in life due to an emotionally violent relationship and needed to recover it. I saw that her boundaries with one son were particularly clouded; I could feel his frustration but it was not with Gina, it was with his father, Gina's ex-husband.

Gina told me that she had indeed come from a very emotionally violent background, with a mother who had consistently humiliated her. When Gina was 11 years old, her mother become an alcoholic after her father died. Gina hadn't thought her childhood was 'that bad' until she had children herself. Her love for her own children had felt very different from what she'd experienced growing up. She then told me that, as I'd seen, she did have a troublesome relationship with one of her sons.

On reflection Gina could see that she'd over-compensated for her ex-husband's moods and aggressive behaviour. And she admitted that she did 'people-please' in order to make others feel okay, over and above her own needs. In order to proceed with her chosen career she'd undertaken numerous training courses, but then decided she needed further qualifications. She now felt she was in a place of stagnation, yet she still had a strong desire to fulfil a sense of purpose.

When we began to explore the origins of the deep anger that Gina couldn't feel, I could sense forming in my mind several images in the area of Gina's chest – they were of white sugar and bread. Gina then told me that when she was growing up in Ireland, sugar sandwiches were often eaten as a meal and she was regularly given them. She then recalled how her angry mother would throw the plate in front of her, demanding she eat the sandwiches. Gina re-experienced the sickness she'd felt back then: not only because of the taste of the sandwiches, but because of the processing of her mother's wrath at the same time.

Gina deduced that her mother must have had a number of emotions going on: a guilt that showed as anger at the fact she was giving her child food of little nutritional value. Gina felt a compassion for her own feelings – the child who was too afraid to speak, too uncertain about expressing her own views in case there was a punishment she felt too uncomfortable to process.

This was translating in Gina's adult life in a similar way, and her sensitive emotions had taken it to a different level with her own son. She decided she had been afraid to define a boundary with him, in case it was translated as being overly strict or aggressive. I suggested she use the intuitive's approach: instead of confronting issues with him, she could instead say, 'Ouch that hurt', when he said or did something inappropriate.

Within a short amount of time Gina's son realized how he'd impacted on her Sensitive nature and he decided to address her differently. They now have a much better understanding of each other. This change of persona had a knock-on effect on the rest of Gina's life.

Today, Gina has a happy relationship with her partner; she has a decent level of communication with him and has learned her own boundaries without having to withdraw from her emotion of anger. After years of stagnating and collecting qualifications, she engaged with working for herself in the holistic field and is now a successful complementary therapist.

Intuitive-Sensitives have a brain advantage

In the course of my work I've seen many different layers of Intuitive-Sensitivity. I've seen it from the earlier stages of psychic fascination through to the engagement of a clearly soul-related healing process (see chapter 9). Throughout, there's always a powerful sense of purpose in resolving past issues and family history, particularly in those whom I would term as Intuitive-Sensitive. There's a strong desire to correct a process where others have either failed or haven't even tried.

Many recognize their own relatives as Sensitive individuals; they can see how their nearest and dearest have similar traits to themselves. But there's a fundamental difference: those relatives haven't engaged their sensitivity – they've either ignored it or hidden it as something to be hopelessly afraid or ashamed of.

The fundamental difference in the Highly Intuitive is intelligence. However, many wouldn't describe themselves as intelligent – in fact, most would say they're the opposite. I wouldn't necessarily define this intelligence as an academic advantage – it's more emotional.

The cerebral cortex is the largest part of the human brain that has developed through evolution. It's the part that distinguishes humans from other animals. It has grown over thousands of years through an increase in neurones and their connections: the number of neurones in the cerebral cortex is therefore a good indicator of intelligence. This evolutionary increase in brain size has improved our information-processing ability and they ways we negotiate relationships within the group.[5]

FMRI scans (Functional Magnetic Resonance Imaging) have shown that Sensitives, when faced with social situations, have more activity in the anterior insula,[6] a part of the cerebral cortex largely associated with empathy, consciousness, self-awareness and emotion.

Meditation is known to have a positive impact on the pre-frontal cortex (part of the cerebral cortex), but I believe the access to it, at a higher level, is through the active development of *intuition*, which is, after all, an exaggeration of the emotions.

I believe there's a trigger within the brain to continue to develop this part of the self, which starts with a need/desire to replace what has been lacking around love. Love, especially for the self, enables us to feel calm, centred and peaceful. Meditation helps us to feel a deeper connection within the self, and therefore a better connection around love for other people. The building of the intuitive process helps us to develop stronger bonds with others because developing intuition leads to a stronger bond with the self.

Having the sense that our intuition is reliable makes us more confident and able to manoeuvre through life's more fast-moving aspects. The rapid pace of modern life has been greatly exaggerated by the advent of technologies such as the internet and social media. Never before have we seen a process develop so quickly, and our minds are having to work harder to keep up. This is therefore pushing for an ever more social brain – one of empathy and emotions, things that come very easily to the Highly Intuitive.

There is, however, an issue: that of the Highly Intuitive Person's past, and their lack of self-worth or self-esteem. As I explained earlier, I believe that these tendencies must have developed at some stage within the earliest foundations, inside the womb and during the formative years of life. They are born, without doubt, from neural stresses at a very early stage of a Highly Intuitive Person's development.

Therefore, in order to feel the calmness and centredness that results from developing their intuitive instincts further, Highly Intuitive People must actively evolve out of their self-esteem issues and into their true feeling of authenticity and personal power, which is as follows:

- A move towards balancing their deepest emotions, and the capability of seeing clearly the processes of others.

- To observe peacefully the interactions of others' emotions, without the belief that they have to process everyone else's world for them, or compensate for other people's anger.

- To accept their levels of empathy as a deep, universal capability that cannot be learned, it can only 'be'.

True feeling and empathy are not skills to be learned: they are natural states only achievable within people who have them. We can learn the essence of an empathetic nature, but we cannot be truly empathetic without an inherent capability for it. In today's world, empathy, conscious connection and human decency are all we have left as unique in a world of instantaneous gratification.

Intuitive-Sensitive People have a unique view of the world

Intuitive-Sensitives can see not only from the emotional world but also from a world of consciousness. There's still a lot of debate about whether consciousness is purely a brain activity or an understanding of something that's wider than human experience is able to comprehend. What I do know, and have certainly seen over the years, is that our inner world shows us what needs healing. It often does this through elaborate symbolism. Sometimes this comes in dreams, and other times it's through events in life.

For example, people often have birds pecking at their window or come across a strangely tame wild bird when they are grieving or need to deal with something particularly emotional. The symbolism here is about having the courage to 'fly'. Or, following a dream, a person can wake up feeling emotional or exhausted, having found themselves revisiting something they haven't thought of in years. It's the psyche's way of showing you what you need to solve now – either the same thing or something that's coming up in life that's very similar.

Once, during a retreat I was teaching, we played a game that involved finding what the group needed to heal by using the words of songs. We did this by letting our minds go blank and quiet, and then asking, in our minds, for a song title to reflect the healing needed. Whoever 'received' a song title first would then Google it, and when the lyrics were viewed, they matched the internal feelings perfectly – in some instances they were spookily accurate. How were they sourced? By asking the internal self to show the symbolism. It never ceases to amaze me how clever our unconscious world is.

The Intuitive-Sensitive's purpose is to evolve beyond their own shadow – to heal aspects of their inherited past and to evolve the best characteristics they can. This, I believe, begins as a spontaneous process; I've never met an Intuitive-Sensitive who consciously chose how they entered the world of their deepest intuition.

As we'll see in the next chapter, the balance of deep emotion (associated with the right-brain) with the logical process (left-brain) will achieve a very peaceful, loving balance in life. All of this is possible, regardless of the Intuitive-Sensitive's early life.

Chapter 4

Intuitive-Sensitivity and Right-Brain Thinking

'I don't believe that consciousness is generated by the brain. I believe that the brain is more of a receiver of consciousness.'

GRAHAM HANCOCK

In his book *A Whole New Mind: Why Right-Brainers Will Rule the Future*, Daniel Pink says: 'Last century, machines proved they could replace human backs. This century, new technologies are proving they can replace human left-brains.'

For years I always got the right-brain/left-brain debate mixed up. Left-brain thinking was said to be more logical, analytical and objective, while the right-brain thinkers were said to be more intuitive, thoughtful and subjective. Which one was I? Was I dominant in the left- or the right-brain? I couldn't remember which way round it was supposed to be. Perhaps this was a subconscious recognition that the division between the brain's hemispheres is a neurological myth.

The left-brain, right-brain argument

The theories around the specialization of the two hemispheres of the brain began in the 1960s when American biologist Roger

W. Sperry and his colleagues conducted so-called 'split-brain' studies on an epileptic patient who'd had his corpus callosum – the 'bridge' between the left and right hemispheres of the brain – split so that the connection was severed. Experimentation showed that certain activities, such as naming objects or putting blocks together in a particular way, could only be done when the patient was using one side of the brain or the other.

Sperry's studies demonstrated that the left side of the brain is normally dominant for analytical and verbal tasks, while the right hemisphere assumes dominance in spatial tasks, music and certain other areas. Today, though, neuroscientists know that the brain has to use *both hemispheres together* in order to perform a wide variety of tasks. The communication between the two hemispheres is reliant on the communication of the corpus callosum, which connects them.

For example, when we listen to someone speaking, the left-side of the brain is picking out the sounds that form the words, while the right-brain is more sensitive to the emotional features of language. In terms of the Intuitive-Sensitive, there's a more natural alignment with the emotional features of language, but it doesn't mean that our left-brain is rejected entirely.

Although various neuroscience studies have established that the brain works as a whole rather than as two halves, and that the right/left-brain debate has nothing left to offer in terms of one having dominance over the other, I believe that the brain of an Intuitive-Sensitive *does* work differently. I believe the notion of left- and right-brain thinking remains highly relevant, especially when we look at certain aspects of the characteristics and traits within human behaviour.

We are not machines, yet today's society demands that of us: it tells us that the brain – and even our intuitive thoughts – are a part of a function that happens purely within the head space. Life is now about indisputable facts, technical processes and the importance of procedures over experience. There's a restriction on other ways of seeing life beyond the parts, and discovering it as a whole. The right-brain is about the 'whole', not parts of it. This is what the Intuitive-Sensitive wants in life: to have the permission to see themselves as the whole. The left-brain-thinking world is about containment, a view from inside the brain and its purely mechanical functions.

When we look at how an Intuitive-Sensitive Person operates, I think the work of the British psychiatrist, doctor and writer Iain McGilchrist speaks to us. He's a strong believer that the right-brain *does* have a significant part to play in how we see life – the colour and the richness of it, and certainly the very human experience of empathy.

He explains how the right frontal lobe has the largest asymmetry in the brain, yet it has been largely ignored as an area of relevance. The truth is, this part of the brain is the basis of our ability to socialize, our connectedness and our empathy. This is the part of us that understands a tone of voice, the subtleness of meaning. It's the part that makes us specifically human.

These are the strongest characteristics of the Intuitive-Sensitive. McGilchrist has a lovely way of putting it: he says the left-brain is about narrowing down to a certainty, while the right-brain is about opening to the less predictable. It's about growing, changing – something that cannot be pinned down.

These are also powerful aspects of the Intuitive-Sensitive – the one thing they cannot stand is being pinned down, tied to something that has no meaning for them. It's what McGilchrist describes as the frontal-lobe expansion: the 'standing back, yet being part of'. And it's what I refer to as the ability to 'observe but not absorb'.

How do you know you're an Intuitive-Sensitive?

Advances in technology, and other huge changes in the way we live our lives, mean that the world is changing rapidly into an environment in which Intuitive-Sensitivity will thrive. The most ideal and exciting time in history for Intuitive-Sensitives is emerging, but before we look into that, it's a good idea to identify the key characteristics of the Intuitive-Sensitive – to recognize the traits you're viewing either within yourself or as you look at another person's behaviour.

As we do this, it's important to remember that a right-brain focused Intuitive-Sensitive likes to see from the whole – to see in, while also standing back. And remember too, that Highly Sensitive People have Sensory Processing Sensitivity[1] – the scientific term for a Sensitive – but not all Sensitives are Intuitive-Sensitive.

Intuitive-Sensitivity requires a level of self-consciousness and a driving inner need to transform aspects of the self around self-esteem and purpose. As an Intuitive-Sensitive you need to be proactive around your own healing requirements, and dynamically involved with your own transformation. Why is this necessary? The desire and the feeling the Intuitive-Sensitive Person wants to get to is a personal nirvana. And that isn't sustainable as an ongoing sensation unless the person willingly works on the self. The feeling of nirvana, peace, tranquillity, happens as part of a self-responsibility: a healthy engagement with transforming rejection – including self-rejection – into love.

Over the years, I've seen countless instances of repeating patterns within the lives of Intuitive-Sensitives who are going through what I refer to as the 'Opening Signs'. I've seen these as patterns that people have not consciously engaged with – they have happened upon them. In some instances I see this as the brain's response to managing stress; in others it can only be some kind of unconscious engagement with the rest of themselves or the mysteries of the grey matter between our ears.

The Opening Signs for Intuitive-Sensitivity

The repeating patterns, or Opening Signs, for Intuitive-Sensitivity shown below don't occur in any particular order. And they don't all have to be there – some disappear, only to return later in life as a person's experiences mature.

- In childhood you knew – but didn't know how you knew – about the secret parts of others' lives.

- You've always been highly perceptive: you can see that the outside of a person doesn't always match the inside. It's obvious to you.

- You know when someone is emotionally upset, even if their outer appearance is happy.

- You find it difficult to compromise yourself – you like the truth of a situation.

- You're very honest and a hopeless liar.

- You're inexplicably drawn to the colours pink, lilac or white.

- You wouldn't define yourself as religious, but you have an interest in something that embraces life in a spiritual way.

- ∾ You find rollercoasters and other high-adrenaline activities stressful.

- ∾ You're uncomfortable with surprises.

- ∾ You've experienced an increase in allergies/food sensitivities, especially gut-related issues.

- ∾ You like fine, beautiful things to look at.

- ∾ You never, if you can help it, sit with your back to a door.

- ∾ When visiting places such as restaurants you always know exactly where the exit is.

- ∾ You're completely exhausted after returning from a shopping trip, yet your companions seem fine.

- ∾ You find yourself, for no particular reason, suddenly easily irritated in the company of other people.

- ∾ You find that high-impact exercise wipes you out for days afterwards.

- ∾ You have a strong need to find purpose. You can't rest without it.

- ∾ You have a large stack of books by the side of your bed that never seems to go down. For important books you'll always have a hard copy; Kindle is for light reading.

- ∾ You find that strangers tell you their life history.

- ∾ You find the truth falls out of your mouth before you can stop it.

- ∾ You avoid confrontation at all costs, unless it involves someone/something incredibly important to you.

∽ You prefer to observe first and talk later.

∽ You're not very good at small talk – you prefer deep conversation.

∽ You're extremely sensitive to others' moods.

∽ You're highly productive in a crisis, when a deeper sense seems to kick in.

∽ You're exhausted around others, yet people are stimulated/animated by your presence.

∽ You're sensitive to medications/have unusual sensitivities.

∽ You're desperate for your work to be of service. If it isn't, you start to feel an urgent need to leave.

The Opening Signs expand further as the intuitive opening process goes deeper for people. They develop into a deeper curiosity that's no longer impacted by fear. At the early stages of the opening process it feels as though your world is changing and it's difficult to stop it. As the opening process goes deeper, you build more confidence in yourself, as it doesn't then feel so outside of your control. You get to the stage where you're choosing to develop your inner world rather than feeling it has chosen you.

For most, the beginning starts with some form of questioning about life – the depth of it and what it means. How you use your time, and questions over whether that's productive, are followed by a strong desire to accumulate knowledge.

Intuitive-Sensitives are very aware of their environment and are social creatures within it, even if their sensitivity takes them into overwhelm. They become hugely frustrated in their work and social environments when they can see a wrong that needs to be corrected, and they will vocalize this, even if it's not popular. The ability to 'see ahead' is obvious to them. They don't understand why someone would fail to change something when they can see it's going to upset the balance of things.

Jessica's story

Jessica and Teresa had been good friends for a number of years. Jessica had often been frustrated by Teresa's irresponsible behaviour but had ignored it, largely because she saw it as part of her friend and that was the way it was.

One summer morning, Jessica received a call from Teresa's teenage son. He was crying. Between the sniffles she could make out that Teresa had got into some kind of argument with her boyfriend. Jessica had met him a handful of times: he seemed to be a pleasant enough man who was always completely charming, but there was something about him she was wary of. She hadn't mentioned this to Teresa, because she seemed so in love with this new relationship, after a failed marriage.

When Jessica arrived at Teresa's house, her friend was quite angry that her son had caused a fuss. She was adamant that everything was fine – the argument was just an argument, the same kind that everyone has. Nevertheless, Jessica stuck around – just to make sure Teresa was okay. She had, though, an overwhelming need to say to Teresa: 'If you don't take this argument as a sign to let this relationship go, you'll get cancer through stress and this man will escalate it to violence. It will happen within a year.' Afterwards, she was very shocked by what she'd said.

Jessica didn't hear from Teresa for some time, and she thought her comment must have upset her friend significantly. It had been after all totally inappropriate, and she didn't know why she'd said it; she just couldn't help herself.

Six months later Jessica received a call from a friend who told her that Teresa had been diagnosed with cancer; she hadn't wished to tell Jessica herself but wanted her to know. The friend also heard how Teresa's boyfriend had been fantastically supportive, helpful and very comforting during her treatment.

Jessica still had a strong feeling of unease about him, though, despite the fact that everything he did to support Teresa was faultless. Another six months later, after Teresa had received successful treatment for the cancer, Jessica took a call from a friend wanting to know if Teresa was okay. She'd heard that Teresa had been involved in a domestic incident and that the police had been called.

Jessica was careful how she approached this news with Teresa, who was now cagey and not very forthcoming about what had happened. It transpired that Teresa was embarrassed. Almost exactly a year after the original argument – and what Jessica had said – the boyfriend did create another incident. He'd become extremely jealous: it seemed that now Teresa was healthy he couldn't cope with it. This time he did escalate it to physical violence; he'd taken it to an incredibly unacceptable level, the police had been called and an arrest was made.

This isn't an unusual example of the process that an Intuitive-Sensitive can go through. They can view a situation from a position of a step back – they can see what they can see. It often becomes awkward for the friend or relative involved, as the information falls out of the Intuitive-Sensitive's mouth before they have the opportunity to stuff it back in.

Jessica couldn't help herself – the information came out before she could filter it adequately. It went on to impact her relationship with her friend, as what she could see seemed very obvious to her, but too scarily accurate for her friend to cope with. Incidents like this make the Intuitive-Sensitive feel as if they are on the periphery of relationships, unsure how they fit in. They feel at home with other people who are as sensitized as they are, but among others, they feel almost unwelcome.

The future belongs to Intuitive-Sensitives

When I tell Intuitive-Sensitive People that they are the next generation of leaders, they aren't sure what I mean. They regard themselves as the troublemakers; the people who state what others want hidden; the ones who aren't very good at playing the political game at home or at work. The last thing they see themselves as is leaders.

In the West, the generation born between 1982 and 2004 is known as the Millennials, and there are 76 million of them. Millennials' views clash significantly with those of the Baby Boomers, the generation born between 1946 and 1964, of which there are slightly more, at 79 million. Stuffed in between the two is Generation X, the individuals born between 1965 and 1979; there are only 51 million of them.

In the workforce, Millennials are often seen as whiny, needy; as seeking constant feedback and immediate gratification. They can multi-task but cannot focus. They are sensitive to criticism and can't work alone. Millennials and Boomers have drastically different views on working life. Boomers have a work ethic of 'work all day and leave it behind when you get home', whereas Millennials see life as one long casual day, and they find it hard to comprehend the idea of the office.

Millennials are uninterested in promotion at work as a definition of their worth, unlike the X-ers, who were the first in the modern era to juggle work with family life. Millennials are motivated by time and flexibility, not money; this keeps them loyal to an employer.[2]

The relevance to the Intuitive-Sensitive of this inter-generational squabbling is that they fit in here very smoothly in terms of leadership.

The world is changing rapidly. We have drastically different economic implications created by the internet, and it's increasingly difficult for the control aspect to continue in the world: the rule of the iron fist will soon become outdated. The economy now demands constant innovation, changes and upgrades, and the rule of the iron fist isn't nimble enough to react quickly.

Millennials are a reflection of this change: they don't have time for the traditional, hierarchical organization, and they believe respect isn't a given, it's something you have to earn. In their world you earn respect by finding the quickest route to a solution, rather than pandering to authority. Their view is that everyone works together, without the old-school rules. The Millennials have a self-confidence and assuredness that puts off older generations, who believe they should have more respect for their elders. The truth is, Millennials don't notice age.

The Boomers were brought up with the notion of a 'job for life', and the idea that you stay in one profession. Millennials cannot and do not have that perspective: they've grown up in a time of extreme change. If an environment doesn't suit their needs, they don't see the point in staying. Generation X find themselves sat somewhere in the middle – they have a bit of both, having grown up in a time pre-technology.

These dramatic differences are shaped by the fact that the Boomers and the Millennials learned about winning in very different circumstances. Boomers learned from the more direct approach of sport and war, while the Millennials have learned from technology: in gaming, if you're losing you reset, so that's what they do – they don't lose, they reset.

Millennials are open to change, because they've always been in it. They're willing and want a balanced life; they've come into a world consumed by instant, ultra-immediate gratification. They've had it all, so the motivation of having it all isn't there. They don't need to win – they want to feel supported, mentored and guided.

By 2025 the majority of employers will be Millennials. The last of the Boomers will be retiring, and the Generation X-ers starting to retire – it will be a new world, an increasingly technology driven one. And that's where the Intuitive-Sensitives come in.

Intuitive-Sensitives, regardless of which generation they sit in, are in a unique position. The Millennials need a softer approach in order to be handled in the workplace. They need a more intuitively sensitive environment to help them to develop the best of their abilities: to understand how they work and the direct needs of the changing world.

Try controlling a teenager today: they're not interested – they answer back and they're not afraid to. They'll generally do anything you ask them, but the key is *asking* – they won't do what they're *told* to. They're no longer ruled by fear, and in many eyes this is the soft touch and makes them unprepared for the realities of the world. The truth is though, that they are prepared: they are prepared for the *new* world.

The Intuitive-Sensitive is the leader within this new world – they bridge the gap. They are the interpreter between the generations, even between their own generation. The world is looking for a gentler, more intuitive touch to get to the key point quicker.

Millennials are becoming more acute in understanding that there's a need to eliminate all unnecessary information, as is the rest of the world. Why? There simply isn't time for it. The intuitive process allows for a quicker access to what's immediately relevant.

The dawning of the Conceptual Age

I love the work of Daniel Pink; in his book *Whole New Mind*, he writes eloquently on the evolution of the Conceptual Age of the 21st century. For more than 100 years – certainly through the Industrial Age (factory workers) and the Information Age (knowledge workers) – we've looked out into the world through the eyes of the left-brain. Life has been sequential, literal, functional and analytical.

Everything developed in recent centuries that's been taken 'seriously' has gone through the mill of 'proof beyond doubt', supported by what we've seen as the functionality of left-brain influence. More right-brain influences, such as seeing the world through the bigger picture – simultaneous, metaphorical, aesthetic and contextual – has been viewed as of much less importance. Until now.

A shift has occurred, or rather, it's in the process of occurring. Access to inexpensive information is already reshaping how we do things: perfectly adequate legal advice can be sourced on the internet; even your washing machine can be fixed with the help of a spanner and YouTube. Anything that a computer can do, or a person in Asia can do for half the price, is now being outsourced to cheaper locations. That's anything that requires functionality, is analytical, sequential or literal.

According to Daniel Pink, we now have the dawning of the 'Conceptual Age': a time where the world's leaders will need to be creators and empathizers. Society is changing – into those who recognize patterns and create meaning. Purpose is making a comeback.

But why is this happening? When the economy and society relied on factories and mass production, right-hemisphere thinking was largely irrelevant. Now we're coming into an age in which the logical process of creation is no longer enough. A passive approach to the development of a working environment is inadequate: there has to be more input.

Technology has made distance irrelevant; we've an abundance of what we need and want, so something has to stand out and it needs to touch the senses – something gentle, yet different, something that a computer can't do. No matter how elaborate technology becomes, a computer cannot truly touch us like another person can; it can't make the wholehearted connection. And no-one can make the wholehearted connection quite like an Intuitive-Sensitive.

Intuitive-Sensitive People in the Conceptual Age

For millions of years human survival has relied on a brain equipped for coping with physical emergencies. The 'fight, flight or freeze' response is still a very real perspective in the world of the Highly Intuitive-Sensitive person – we know that one well. We're very much in touch with our sympathetic nervous system and particularly our limbic reactions. Most Intuitive-Sensitives have an elephant's memory for emotional stimulation, recalling in minute detail the long-term effects of particular life events.

Many (myself included) can recall events in life during the infant years. I shocked my mother once by recalling the exact layout of a house we lived in for the first three years of my life. I even gave accurate information about the day we moved in, when I was aged three: who looked after the children, what we did, the fact it was raining and that we wore bright yellow raincoats. I also told her the make and colour of the car my father had when we lived there and the day they went to collect her Siamese cat, Ming.

Such an ability to recollect is both a blessing and a hindrance. For the Intuitive-Sensitive, memories remain vivid, often for longer than we'd like them to. Give a Intuitive-Sensitive something emotional to recall, and we're straight back there: pictures, music, feelings, often the whole bundle.

In previous eras, emotional input, or indeed outpourings, were seen as a weakness in the workforce; a Sensitive's emotional hyper-sensitivity was sidelined for a more 'practical' intellect-based, level-headed approach. However, the advent of the Conceptual Age – triggered by technological changes, economic requirements and consumer saturation – means that emotions, creativity, vivid thinking and intuition are the new fashion. The sensitivity we've been brought up to believe we need to toughen up on is now here for the long-haul.

According to Claudio Fernández-Aráoz, author of the article '21st-Century Talent Spotting' featured in *Harvard's Business Review*, what comes naturally to an Intuitive-Sensitive Person are the qualities of the successful leaders of the future. The right skills are no longer enough – it's the ability to master new ones coupled with the ability to naturally develop emotional relationships with people that counts. There has to be a level of emotional flexibility, understanding and empathic creativity.

Fernández-Aráoz says the leaders of the modern business world will need the skills of motivation – beyond self-ambition and more directed to the good of the whole. This means that what many have seen as corporate selfishness – stepping over people – just won't cut it any more.

Intuitive-Sensitive People find the ruthless approach of upsetting others intensely distressing. They often find themselves in a position of dealing with predatory individuals within the workplace, but cannot, no matter how much they are expected to, actively behave in an offensive way to others.

Another point Fernández-Aráoz makes is how the new market is looking for curiosity – an openness to new experiences and information. Curiosity is a Highly Intuitive-Sensitive person's middle name: without it they would not be intuitive. The intuitive instinct is developed through an inner drive for expansion and a nosy attitude.

The third aspect is engagement on a new level. The leaders of the future will need the ability to connect with people both emotionally and logically. Highly Intuitive People, when in their element, have a passion and enthusiasm for what they do. They like the opportunity to draw people towards team efforts, kindness and encouragement, but currently often lack belief in their ability to do this. They may shy away from being the centre of attention, preferring to be cheering from the wings.

The fourth and final aspect is determination and the ability to push towards difficult goals, take on challenges and recover quickly from setbacks. In the first instance, an Intuitive-Sensitive Person may look for the safer option; however, in my experience of them, if they have a passion, and are driven by the good of the whole, determination is the least of their worries. Their drive, through the deeper self-faith component, is a hugely stimulating factor for change as they make their way to the finish line.

I've seen many of my Intuitive-Sensitive clients transform and grow through their intuitive abilities. They've already embracing the merits of the new world leadership. I've seen their inner belief, capabilities and natural talent for engaging the co-operation of others flower into amazing achievements.

I've seen their bank balances grow enormously, too, through promotions, work adjustments and following their real passion in life. I've seen them offered huge pay rises, amazing placements and things that have made their colleagues green with envy.

How? Why? What were they doing?

They shifted their thinking from seeing their intuitive nature as something embarrassing and pointless to using it productively in their choices. They began to learn how to control the emotional component of intuitive ability out of their fears and into their own power. They no longer saw it as something freaky – they transformed the earlier foundations of criticism and rejection into self-acceptance for the inspiration of others.

In essence, the desire for inclusion is finally here to be fulfilled. It's the Intuitive-Sensitive's time. We're here, in an era when high-tech isn't enough. We're in what Daniel Pink refers to as the 'high concept/high touch' era. High concept is the ability to create artistic and emotional beauty, while high touch involves the ability to empathize, to understand the subtleties of human interaction, to stretch towards purpose and meaning.

Pink uses the examples of medical schools to illustrate this point. Medical environments are the last place we expect anything other than logic to reside. He says: 'More than fifty medical schools across the United States have incorporated spirituality into their coursework.' Has the world of medicine suddenly become woo-woo? No, it hasn't, but there's a growing realization that empathy and intuition are areas no amount of technology or diagnostic tools can teach, yet they are highly desired attributes.

Elsewhere, businesses are realizing the way to sell their goods and services is to make them stand out in today's overstocked marketplace. Pink says they're having to do this by making what they offer physically beautiful and emotionally connecting. He says: 'Today we're in the art business.' And that's a perfect world for those who feel in a deep way, know how people work, are intuitively aware in their environment and are creative and powerfully sensitive.

This means that, as an Intuitive-Sensitive, instead of focusing on trying to be different to how you are, you can focus on being more of who you are. We're in the habit of trying to hide our sensitivity and certainly our intuitive focus, especially in the workplace. The new way will mean that our talents – our gentle nature, which seems to see patterns before they've formed, our ability to talk to the most challenging person with ease because somehow we just know that's what they want – will be more commonly desired and utilized in the workforce.

Chapter 5

Recognizing the Opening Process

'We always know which is the best road
to follow, but we follow only the road
that we have become accustomed to.'
PAULO COELHO

The chitchat; the eyes darting from one direction to another, working out who's worth talking to; an unspoken ban on discussing anything that reaches deeper than the surface; the power plays of who does what for a living; the fake laughter; the over-enthusiastically gripped handshakes followed by inane references to the weather.

In many social gatherings, you'll see the Intuitive-Sensitive hanging back; they are last to enter the room in the hope that those who go before them get the initial meeting and greeting over and done with so they don't have to.

There are some kinds of normal social interaction that most Intuitive-Sensitives will do their best to avoid. They keep their distance not because they're shy but because the processing of what feels fake to them is too hard to bear. It feels like an invasion – to some extent as though the door opens and they must brace themselves for the bucket of mud thrown at them.

Sensitive people live their life in preparation: the more Sensitive they are, especially to the vibrational adjustments of people, their mindsets and general feelings, the more they have to prepare themselves in the social world. Sensitive people are often mistaken as shy – their desire to hang back being seen as a lack of initiative and confidence – or at times, rude.

The truth is they're neither of these things. Instead, they are overwhelmed by the processing of others in the room and are easily tongue-tied by superficial conversation. This is because they can see and feel what's *not* being said. They sense the undertones of a conversation – they can even, to a certain extent, feel the *thoughts* running through the heads of those present. And this energy is both off-putting and highly distracting.

Seeing beyond the mask

Like most Intuitive-Sensitive People, when I was a child I could easily see the mask people presented to the world. I could see beyond their mask of confidence to what lay underneath. For some it was a deep insecurity, for others it was a fear of being revealed. As a child though, I was never sure what they thought might be revealed. I learned to repress this instinct and to never bring it up, until at last adult life forced it to the surface.

For many Intuitive-Sensitive People, the opening process to the deeper side of the self begins with a desire to escape the mask in all areas of life. The Opening Signs (see chapter 4) force much of this to the surface. The feeling you know but don't know how you know, about the secret parts of people's lives; knowing when someone is upset even if their outer world looks sunny; the difficulty in compromising yourself; these are all parts of the opening process and the revealing of the mask.

There comes a time when deeper connections are no longer just a nice idea – they are a necessity. The ability to gloss over things, to engage in small talk, becomes not only less appealing, but less possible. It's at this point that the Intuitive-Sensitive begins to feel out of place in the world, isolated from their environment. For many it feels somehow their responsibility to ease the mask of others' shame and take the responsibility themselves. This is the point where the opening process deepens into a changing world they can't control.

If you're a Sensitive, there's a feeling of getting the measure of everyone you meet, very quickly. There's a feeling of knowing people instantly, yet they don't seem to know *you*. They don't notice the subtleties of who you are, and you feel wounded because you can see what's important to them. Superficiality isn't something you can maintain, yet to you it feels as though the world demands it.

In my experience, for the Intuitive-Sensitive to develop there has to be a period of separation – the ability to step back into a place of neutral observation in order to see more clearly and to neutralize the desperate experience of emotional overload.

The beginning of this journey can feel lonely. The vast majority of people cannot see the mask a person presents – they rely only on their verbal communication, body language and tone of voice. For the Intuitive-Sensitive, seeing something deeper is uncomfortable, as others are blissfully unaware of the things that we see as obvious.

To picture it, we look beyond the 'mask' of the serene swan to notice that the legs are paddling like mad beneath the surface. The issue is that all humans want you to see is the serene glide – that, after all, is the only thing anyone else notices. Sometimes they're unnerved that you can see the real work happening, and they try their best to distract you from it.

This is deeply confusing to the Intuitive-Sensitive Person's inner world. They see a fine mask of perfection in a person, yet a crumbling inner world. But if they ask any questions they are met with a curt, defensive response because the person feels their weakness is somehow exposed for all to see.

The question is: How do we deal with these feelings? How do we recognize and prevent them from negatively impacting us? We learn how to control the more basic part of how we define ourselves, and this is done by understanding our less developed parts of the self – the internal 'gremlins' and 'goblins'.

Our brain's 'computer' and its gremlins and goblins

In his book *The Chimp Paradox*, sports mind doctor Dr Steve Peters explains effectively the main thing the Intuitive-Sensitive wants to solve in life as part of their process of realizing they're opening to their deeper world. He describes it as the case of 'computers, goblins and gremlins'.[1]

In Peters' concept, the computer is the guiding influence in the brain, and when working well, it gives the mind stability. He says that when we're born, the computer is an empty hard drive, ready for the storage of the beliefs and behaviours we gather as we go through life. I believe it's a little more complicated than that – due to the minefield of issues passed down through the generations – but we'll look at that later.

The computer stores the information of the 'autopilot' – the positive beliefs and automatic functions placed in our behavioural system (the computer) throughout our life that help us to be successful and happy. And it also stores what Peters calls 'gremlins' and 'goblins'. Gremlins are unhelpful or destructive beliefs or behaviours. These are wired into the brain after the age of eight and are more associated with what we know to be removable – how we look out into the world with temporary frustrations, show a lack of commitment to a particular outcome or procrastinate over decisions.

The goblins are the tricky beliefs, as they are much more difficult to remove. They require a lot of conscious realization and active participation with our internal world. Goblins are programmed into the computer *prior* to the age of eight, and are more or less associated with the unconscious aspects of 'worth'. An example would be how a person associates his or her worth in the world with parental approval and how that found its way into the computer.

It's the goblins in other people that the Intuitive-Sensitive can see the most. People are generally blissfully unaware of their goblins and how they interact in the outer world, but the Intuitive-Sensitive individual is incredibly aware of them, especially when they see a room full of them.

In the early days of the opening process they don't know what to do with them – how to handle them or whether to even mention them. When this is mixed with the Intuitive-Sensitive's own goblins, then inner hell breaks loose.

From what I've seen over the years this is often the trigger point for a strong spiritual connection. This is by no means religious; it's a connection to something bigger than the individual, a developing faith in the inner world. I see this as necessary for the 'computer' to maintain balance between all the components it's managing. It's as though the computer is indeed not a machine, but conscious. It develops a spiritual connection, or opens it up, in order to protect the whole from being overwhelmed.

Managing our gremlins and goblins

As the opening process continues, the Intuitive-Sensitive becomes more sensitized to other people and their inner world, and as they develop their skills, the ability to manage superficial 'fluff' becomes increasingly difficult to cope with. They begin to feel completely exhausted around other people, and need to prepare themselves for certain situations and environments. This isn't to say their system is weak: it's simply burdened.

They then begin to search for authentic relationships based on kindness and honesty. The airs and graces of superiority and inferiority become overwhelmingly tiring and stressful for the Sensitive, mostly because the processing of their own gremlins and goblins is enough to deal with, without the projections of other people's. I often see at this stage a Sensitive soul going into a stage of withdrawal to recover; the withdrawal aspect is the inner world – often at an unconscious level – deciding it needs to rebalance the situation.

In my experience, developing your intuition helps the computer manage the gremlins and goblins. When we become more aware of the programming in our inner computer it makes it much easier to observe rather than feel completely absorbed by a situation. Intuition makes us more aware of when something is changing. And if we're more aware of what's in our own system, we get to notice a gremlin and goblin tantrum coming before it's in full flow.

Developing our intuition so we can notice the gremlins and goblins before they get out of hand means nurturing our ability to feel. The next time you feel agitated or frustrated, take a moment to ask yourself: *What am I really feeling?* Feel through your body, not your head space. Gremlins and goblins take over the head space, intuition takes over the body space.

It's at this stage we're able to develop a true compassion and empathy for others and their often out-of-control inner world, rather than seek to reject all that enters our over-stimulated inner experience. When gremlins and goblins are able to articulate their feelings and emotional reactions, they don't need to push for some attention.

Lisa's story

Lisa's early experiences of relationships had been marked by inconsistency. She would either meet partners who were overly attentive and desperate, or those who were emotionally distant. She'd find herself becoming annoyed and irritated around the attentive ones, even though they were perfectly pleasant, but she'd be heavily into the emotionally distant ones. Lisa began, therefore, to have the reputation among her friends of following the 'bad boys' – finding herself in relationships with them one after another.

When Lisa got married, in her early thirties, she thought she'd cracked it. In her husband, a seemingly quietly attentive person, she believed she'd finally found happiness. It wasn't long though before she increasingly experienced both her goblins and gremlins on high alert. She found herself working late more often, pushing for more success, going out for drinks with colleagues, and generally avoiding her husband.

Lisa was shocked by her behaviour. By the time she asked me about it, her life had sunk into embarrassing drunken evenings she felt powerless to stop. She told me it was too painful to be as Sensitive as she was. She felt her world was about to explode with overwhelm. I asked her what her inner world was trying to say. Her inner world answered: having come from a family where she felt rejected, she couldn't cope with another bout of it from the man she loved. In short, her goblins and gremlins were trying to create rejection, before she was rejected.

Lisa had picked up intuitively that her husband was not the man she thought him to be. His inner world was decidedly chilly, his outer full of charm. He'd never shown her any physical unkindness, just a coolness. Her goblins and gremlins were trying to tell her, 'You're not worthy of love, which is why you've picked a man who can never show you what you need.'

Lisa allowed herself to feel rather than intellectualize her feelings. She allowed herself to feel in the body; she heaved uncontrollable tears with a deep, deep sadness and a grief for her lost early life with a mother who couldn't show affection, only approval for achievement. The tears were the little girl, the goblin entrenched and hard-wired into her system that she was not worthy unless she achieved.

I continued to see Lisa for a considerable time afterwards. I helped her process her emotions through an amicable divorce. Her goblins and gremlins now able to speak – to voice their upset – managed to release graciously, rather than punish, her husband. I felt strongly, intuitively, she would meet the right person for her quite quickly; it was almost as though her real husband was waiting in the wings. She took a while to let go of her ex-husband – it took time because she needed to release gently; recovering her worthiness was not an overnight job. Her goblins needed to see a safe outcome before they would properly let go.

Within a few months Lisa met a lovely man. Today, they are happily married: he loves her dearly and she loves him. They have a freedom and level of communication in their relationship that's refreshing to see as a true partnership.

Dr Peters says that the world of the goblin cannot be changed. It's hard-wired into the brain, deep in our psyche, as our foundational experiences prior to the age of eight. It can only be negotiated around, contained, not solved. Although I believe this to be true in the majority of cases, I've seen how considerable change in this area does occur in Highly Intuitive-Sensitive People, the more conscious and self-responsible they become.

Managing our monkey mind

The monkey mind is the everyday self, powered by primal instincts. It likes praise; it likes to be recognized in the external world and valued by other people for its achievements in life. Figuring what's a plus and what's a minus, feeling empathic and conscientious isn't part of the monkey mind – it has an agenda and that's power in the external world: to feel in control, recognized and to a certain extent superior. This is especially the case in people who have a very active monkey mind. We all know a few of them!

The monkey mind needs a role in life in which it has an essence of territory. This is a primal requirement from our earliest roots; it's not a choice we make, it comes from the instinct to protect the species. In males it's to fight boundaries, in females it's to defend the home/nest.[1] If the monkey doesn't have territory it starts to feel insecure; it has a tantrum and looks for attention.

Intuitive-Sensitive People spend their lives trying to tame other people's monkeys. They feel the primal rising of the baboon hitting its chest and it scares them. The monkey in another person may not have shown the fullness of its tantrum in the external world, but the Intuitive-Sensitive Person can immediately feel it building for the journey out.

The feeling and the instinct in the Intuitive-Sensitive is to quickly do what's necessary to suppress the wrath of someone else's monkey. Often, it will be to immediately and unexplainably play a submissive role, one that will later really annoy them. They may usually be articulate, quick to defend what they need to defend within themselves, but somehow, much to their annoyance, other people can turn them into a blubbering, gibbering wreck with a swish of their monkey tail.

This is partly why Intuitive-Sensitives cannot handle confrontation well. They don't want to deal with an out-of-control monkey – they have no desire to try to control it, only to protect their boundary if necessary.

The issue is that too much time is spent concentrating on making sure everyone else's monkey is happy. This exhausts the Intuitive-Sensitive to the point that they feel no-one cares for *their* wellbeing. This is the stage at which their own monkey starts kicking off: not in other people's direction, though, it kicks off towards the self. It starts to demand more and wants your attention. To get this, it will, in the beginning, set about unconsciously poking at the territory of other monkeys, by trying to reason with them.

The monkey mind doesn't respond to reasoning: it responds to nurturing. It's child-like, self-orientated and looks dumbly at your reasoning. It then jumps up and down, screaming in your face. Intuitive-Sensitives are always shocked when I say, 'Start communicating; say what you want. Say it from a neutral perspective.' How do you achieve that neutral perspective? You nurture your own monkey first; well looked after, nurtured monkeys do as they're asked.

In the early days of the opening process, it's easy to see when you're beginning to nurture your monkey. You stop trying to control everyone else's and the pleasing aspect goes out of the window. This is the stage of saying, 'Goodbye manipulation' and it's a necessary part of the long-term development cycle.

Nurturing your own monkey means building it a home. Many Intuitive-Sensitive people have no idea where they fit in: they develop a compulsion to move. During events, when I ask the question 'How many of you feel stuck and think it's time to move?' the number of hands that go up is astounding.

Sensitives often feel they need to move home, location, their job and often the very foundations of their life. The truth is the searching doesn't satisfy the inner need. This is because it's the monkey who thinks changing something on the outside is going to impact the inner and make it feel safe. What the monkey is actually asking for is its home, the foundations it would like to help it satisfy its primal need for territory.

The 'monkey home' is about creating a safe place to feel nurtured. If you had a good foundation early in life, then nurturing your monkey is much easier, simply because the primal foundations were more easily established. If you didn't, then your monkey will feel it needs to be on the move and looking for new environments to find its place to settle.

The disappointment builds through life, as more and more locations and changes do not seem to satisfy it. What it's actually asking for is that you look *inwards*, to nurture it so it feels safe. When that happens, it's less likely to attract other screaming monkeys.

Anna's story

Anna was used to moving home every three to five years. At around the second year of living in a house she'd start to get itchy feet, which would then develop into an unbearable desire to scratch, usually at the end of the third, and certainly going into the fourth year.

When I spoke to her, she was very close to completing the third year of living in her current house, and I had the impression that she'd moved numerous times before. The itchiness of her desire to consistently move on seemed obvious in the attentiveness of her behaviour and her urgency around questions and 'complete' answers. She also seemed very uncomfortable with leaving anything in life in the lap of the gods.

Anna had fallen in love with a quiet man. Brian was a gentle, kind soul, but always emotionally distant. One moment he'd show Anna quite a lot of affection, but this would be closely followed by periods of emotional distance. When questioned, Brian didn't know what Anna was talking about. Anna had learned to live with and accept that Brian was attentive sometimes and distant the rest of the time. He was never unpleasant, and she became used to this imbalance in their relationship.

Anna admitted she'd always been clingy in her relationship with Brian. This annoyed her, she said, because she wasn't the clingy type; she described herself as self-sufficient. Yet Brian brought something out in her, making her very emotionally demanding. They'd dated for years before Brian had finally asked her to marry him, and they'd been married for 16 years. I asked Anna how she felt about Brian now. She became a little prickly and defensive when I asked that, rather than answering her question about why she wanted to keep moving. 'Our marriage is fine; I just want to move,' she replied. But rather than returning to the moving issue, I gently asked Anna about her early life and her father.

She said that her father was a lovely man, kind and gentle, but for as long as she could remember, he'd had this dark cloud of emotional avoidance. When she'd go to him for comfort, he would quietly make excuses and refer Anna to her mother, or he'd give her something to do. Anna felt this was his way of helping her in life – to become self-sufficient and anything but needy.

Anna's father had lost his own father at a very young age – he'd died during World War II – and as a child he learned never to rely on anyone. He became very self-sufficient, especially when his mother was forced to work several jobs to keep the family.

Anna's father had used this method of self-sufficiency as a means of self-protection. When someone came too close, he'd back off in a practical way. This had taught Anna's monkey to scream at another monkey when affection was part of the mix, but never to communicate it. Anna's screaming monkey, and its insecurity, was shown through the desire to move. When it would build to an uncomfortable level, Anna would put the house up for sale.

Anna had been attracted to Brian as an unconscious extension of what she was used to around love. Her monkey had learned that 'love means occasional affection, followed by rejection'. This had become something that Anna's own monkey was feeling from her. The new home would provide the occasional affection, which would soon wear off.

Her monkey then needed a new home to at least feel temporarily nurtured. Even though Anna was still married to Brian, it had felt to me as though they were no longer together. The distance had grown to the extent that Brian's monkey was screaming through a lack of communication altogether. His had taken the constant house moving to mean what he provided wasn't good enough.

I asked Anna to sit and feel in her body – just for the moment – her upset around Brian's lack of affection. I then asked her at the same time to feel her father's avoidance around affection. This took her a while to do, as she'd never really allowed herself access to it before. When she felt it, her inner child-self cried like a baby. An outpouring she never knew was there. When the crying had finished, I asked her if she still needed to move. Her instant reply was, 'No, not at all, I've a very nice home.'

In that moment Anna had become consciously aware of what her monkey was looking for, and had begun the process of addressing a long-held goblin. In nurturing her own monkey – by acknowledging that something in her distant past had upset it and how her present was triggering it – she was able to settle it to the extent that she could calmly go to Brian for communication.

Without either of them feeling cornered, and with Anna's monkey calm, the couple were able to have an honest conversation. Brian confessed that he'd never felt 'enough' in his own life. Both his parents had been highly critical of him when he was a child; he felt this had made him conscious of how to be kind to people, yet he couldn't accept kindness himself. He felt that Anna was quick to say how dissatisfied she was with her life, and he felt he was somehow responsible. He wanted to reach out to her, but experienced what he described as a 'horrendously bad mood' every time he tried to do so. He hoped, he said, to be able to manage it better now.

Anna, as the Intuitive-Sensitive one in this relationship will find it easier to become more conscious of the monkey. Having experienced it so clearly through her emotions, she'll feel better able to acknowledge it when it feels agitated. Practise will help her keep a quiet, nurtured monkey, until the intuitive part of who she is grows to the extent the nurtured monkey becomes the norm. She'll then need to spend less time trying to settle it.

For the Intuitive-Sensitive trying to keep others' monkeys from screaming and jumping in your face is no easy feat. The problem arises if you're only temporarily nurturing your own monkey. Intuitive-Sensitives look always to see where someone else's monkey needs nurturing; they see it as their job to calm it down, and they think it's their responsibility to solve it.

Anna, following her conversation with Brian, will think it's up to her to help Brian to keep his monkey's screaming in check; to help him feel less vulnerable in the world when his monkey is upset. She'll seek to pacify it, rather than see it as his responsibility. The key is, if you can help, then help; if you can't, you walk away from a screaming monkey and let it calm down. What makes it calm down? Allowing it to feel what the emotion is. Intuitive-Sensitives find it hard to walk away; however, they have an empathetic compulsion to fix an out-of-control monkey and feel it's somehow their fault.

Giving your monkey what it needs

Nurturing your monkey, and therefore allowing your gremlins and goblins their say so they can let go of controlling your inner world, is essential for the wellbeing of an Intuitive-Sensitive. If your internal world is too full of others' energy to process, it will start backing up into overwhelm and overload. This is the point at which your energy will attract uncomfortable lessons, rather than the clearer world of insight.

If your monkey is insecure, it isn't well managed; if it hasn't got a clearly defined territory, it'll attract predators, who are very attracted to the empathetic nature of the Intuitive-Sensitive (we look in depth at the role of the predator in chapter 7). This is because Highly Intuitive-Sensitive People don't generally have an aggressive and dominant monkey – it tends to be on the submissively insecure side, rather than assault provoking if it doesn't have territory.

What has actually happened is your monkey, wandering around searching, hasn't a 'home' within. It's therefore vulnerable to persuasion – a promise of nurturing and the deeply intuitive part of the internal world is parked to one side. Why? The monkey isn't intuitive; it needs to feel nurtured in order for the intuitive aspect of consciousness to come forward, to establish itself beyond the rational, everyday component. An increasingly insecure monkey, feeling abandoned, will go for whatever promises an instant fix.

I have a very sad story to tell of such an encounter. The purpose of sharing this isn't to frighten, it's to highlight the extremity of such a situation. Debbie was a lovely person who came to one of my workshops in 2008 and then joined my online support environment for Sensitives as a member in 2009.

Debbie, whose nickname was 'Debbie from Nottingham', attended every online session; she was extremely active within the group and asked a lot of questions. In one live session, which I remember vividly, she told me she'd met a man who'd asked her to marry him. She was delighted and wanted to share her happiness. I'd seen her recently, as she'd just attended an event I'd hosted in London. Though her words were excited, my heart and face sank at the mention of this man.

I felt very strongly that his core was dark, cold and dangerous: even though I had never met or seen him. I tried to tell Debbie to ease up, to let the relationship go on for longer before committing to marriage. She wasn't keen on this idea and became slightly hostile, so I left it and moved on to the next question.

The next live session came and went, and there was no 'Debbie from Nottingham'. I began to think my comment had upset her. I'd heard that her boyfriend had moved in with her, so I assumed she was otherwise occupied. I still had an ongoing feeling of unease, but could do nothing about it. I knew the wedding was due to take place shortly.

I never heard from Debbie again, although she didn't formally cancel her membership. I thought it was very strange – out of character – but assumed her new husband didn't approve of her dalliance with my membership group. For quite some while, I would periodically think of her and wonder how she was getting along.

Then, one day in January 2013, as I was waiting for a flight at London Gatwick Airport, I had an extremely vivid picture come into my mind of 'Debbie from Nottingham'; I recognized her curly brown hair and big smile. Once again I wondered how she was getting along.

A few weeks later, I received a somewhat cryptic message from another member, asking me if I remembered 'Debbie from Nottingham' and saying that something had happened to her, but she couldn't at that moment elaborate. Debbie and this person had become good friends through my membership group; she had been a witness at her wedding. I answered with a handful of sentences, pretty much saying, 'I know she's gone and that he did it.'

Jamie Starbuck was convicted of Debbie's murder in May 2013. She'd not been seen alive since a few days after her wedding in April 2010. Starbuck had murdered her, disposed of her and gone around the world having stolen a chunk of her inheritance. Friends and family believed Debbie was off travelling for two years with her new husband. Messages would regularly come from her email account, telling them about their trips and destinations.

The time I had seen her face at London Gatwick Airport was the same time and day that Jamie Starbuck was arrested at London Heathrow Airport, after returning on a flight from Brazil. He is now serving a minimum of 30 years' imprisonment.

I was deeply saddened by the grotesque death of such a lovely person; Debbie was a delightful, gentle soul and most certainly an Intuitive-Sensitive. But why did her intuition let her down? If I could see Starbuck's darkness despite having never met him, spoken to him or heard anything but pleasant things about him, how could *she* not see it?

Part of the reason was the monkey – that primitive component of Debbie's mind was desperate to feel nurtured, so it accepted this masked view of love. She hadn't found her 'home' – in the group she'd often say that she wasn't sure where to settle, where to set her roots, as she wanted to be certain of her purpose before deciding. A monkey without a feeling of nurturing and 'home' can become easily manipulated.

Protecting your monkey by offering it the basis of what it wants, to feel settled, happy and comfortable in its metaphorical cage, helps to protect it from believing that all that glitters is gold. It protects it from suspicion, closed-mindedness and most importantly of all, the manipulation of those who exercise a darkness in life. Darkness is the absence of light. Light is the building of our Intuitive-Sensitive muscle into something we respect rather than reject in ourselves.

Chapter 6

Why Intuitive-Sensitive People Need Purpose

'Concepts without intuitions are empty,
intuitions without concepts are blind.'
IMMANUEL KANT

Regardless of the ways in which their goblins, gremlins and monkey mind work, Intuitive-Sensitives feel a need for their life to contain a significant level of purpose. The management of the monkey mind is an ongoing challenge, one that takes conscious effort and recognition. Purpose, though, is different.

All the people I've engaged with over the years who have a noticeably higher sense of sensitivity and a natural feel for things haven't the capacity for extensive small talk, but they do need to feel quietly connected at all times.

As we learned earlier in the book, people with high levels of intuitive insight have often, though not always, come from a foundational background that featured a significant level of criticism or extensive rejection. There's something different in their nature that bores a deep hole in others' psyches. It's as though they've been able to look deeply into another's soul – and this spooks other people.

Emotionally badly behaved adults will feel an Intuitive-Sensitive's energy and try to destroy their curiosity at an early age. The intuitive child will realize this, though, and seek to work around it. They'll have methods of adjusting to their environment that go beyond logic, but they will perhaps have been told from a young age that some part of them is fundamentally stupid.

This is where I've seen – as the intuitive nature comes back into its time to flourish – a very strong desire to find a sense of purpose. It's a driving need to dissolve the indoctrination that they are daft, wrong – and that their intuitive input is irrelevant.

This isn't the case with all Intuitive-Sensitive People: not all have the job of resolving early-life dysfunction; some are lucky enough to have side-stepped that lesson. However, most who are committed to their long-term inner development, and feel a strong force to find purpose, will have this fundamental issue as a driving influence.

I can almost guarantee that when an Intuitive-Sensitive Person wants to take their understanding beyond the basics of figuring out what being intuitive means, engage their purpose and live a life committed to some sort of transformation, their family history involves psychological unpredictability impacting on emotions. Part of their ongoing drive for purpose is about making a profound difference to their inner world and outer influence; this is in part due to a deep desire to heal the family lineage.

Kathy's story

I've known Kathy for many years. I've seen her inner world go through various ups and downs, but she's always stoical and strong. She has a thriving small business with more clients than she can ever handle, as her meticulous approach and attention to detail is highly regarded. Kathy has plenty of freedom – she works for herself; her business has bounced along perfectly through a recession, and she's very intuitively sensitive to her clients' requirements.

However, Kathy suffers from a recurring pattern that looks very much like 'Impostor Syndrome': a psychological phenomenon that impacts successful women in particular. And there's a raging outbreak of it among Intuitive-Sensitives! Impostor Syndrome is where people cannot internalize their accomplishments and believe that some day they are going to be exposed as a fraud; proof of their success is dismissed and trivialized. We'll look at this in more depth in Chapter 7.

Kathy is brilliant at disregarding her accomplishments and stuffing them to one side. She's consistently looking: searching for a sense of connection and purpose. Kathy cannot see that she's already contributing, accessing a level of purpose that fits very nicely with the fundamental make-up of an Intuitive-Sensitive.

Kathy is the eldest child, the one who for years put to one side the family dysfunction through loyalty and duty. Kathy's father has been an alcoholic for as long as she can remember. She once described him to me as a 'heavy drinker', before admitting that his habits had been present since her childhood. This meant that when she was young, he was drunk, angry or never available.

Her mother was a gentle character who tried to protect the family as best she could. But she had her own secret – one that she only revealed to Kathy on her deathbed. She'd had another child, a son she'd given up at birth – a foundational shame she could not communicate. The secret had kept her emotionally withdrawn from her two other children, Kathy and her sister.

I suspect that Kathy had taken on the emotional responsibility of the family secret: the hidden world she had little (father's addiction) to no knowledge of (mother's secret). This has created a tucked-in world for Kathy, where she feels that no matter what she achieves, she's a fraud, an impostor waiting to be found out.

Part of Kathy's purpose, therefore, will be to heal this family cycle, a situation she has a tremendous amount of empathy for, but can't shake off as her responsibility. Kathy's lesson is to realize what she carries isn't hers to carry. Her caring, lovely nature doesn't make it necessary for her to shoulder her mother's burden, or to protect her father from his addiction for the foreseeable future. Her 'purpose' therefore, is to hand the responsibility to those whose energy it is, hence the reason a sense of unfulfilled 'purpose' will chase her until she learns to give the burden up.

Right-brain, left-brain and the pursuit of purpose

To the Intuitive-Sensitive, purpose is more than just purposeful work. It's about changing their own history, re-writing it. It's about spiritual insights, an access to their own truth, and clarity; resolving what they 'should' expect of themselves based on earlier conditioning. It's about access to introspection, replacing fear with love and protecting themselves from rejection (mostly self-rejection). It's about adjusting guilt – as a fear of the past and anxiety – as fear in the present. It's also a deeply held truth of the right-brain influence.

I believe there are answers to be found in looking again at the right- and left-brain, their connections and differences, via the work of Iain McGilchrist. He explains beautifully the dynamic of the two hemispheres and how it impacts the world of the Intuitive-Sensitive.

As we learned earlier, the neurological debate about left- and right-brain dominance has long been abandoned, due to the realization that the hemispheres work together. It's not true that one part of the brain does reason and the other emotion, which was a popular concept up until recent times. In fact, both sides of the brain are very much engaged with reason and emotion.

McGilchrist says that the left hemisphere is concerned with precise, simplified information; it has a narrow, sharply focused attention to detail. He uses a perfect example of how a bird, while pecking, needs to know the exact spot to peck among an area of grit to pick up the food bits. The clever part is, while it's doing this, it still has to be broadly aware of its environment, so it can see what's approaching and identify potential predators.

It's the right hemisphere that has the broad, open approach. It takes in the whole, rather than parts. It's open, vigilant and alert. This difference is known because patients who have lost their right hemisphere (an example would be a stroke) experience a pathological narrowing of focus. It's this right-hemisphere identification that gives us an insight into what makes Intuitive-Sensitive people tick – and their drive for purpose. The right hemisphere is 'broadly vigilant' and Intuitive-Sensitives are more than this – they are *hyper-vigilant*.

Let's return to the pecking bird: it's concentrating on eating, yet at the same time, it's aware of its wider environment. Intuitive-Sensitives tend to have come from a disruptive environment – perhaps one that featured emotional violence, unpredictability, or at least a generational history that related to punishment. These early issues have perhaps increased the right-brain training in terms of vigilance, or indeed, hyper-vigilance.

The right-brain and the desire for freedom

As I mentioned earlier, I've yet to meet an Intuitive-Sensitive who, on entering a room or an unfamiliar place, doesn't immediately figure out where the exit is, or position themselves facing the door. Some are also reluctant and cautious around social situations that involve sitting at a long table rather than a round one. This fear seems illogical to them, and they struggle to figure out why they have it.

The issue comes from the fact that a long table suggests that someone will have to head it, become the dominant figure. Therefore the Intuitive-Sensitive will possibly have to energetically fend off a control environment, rather than just relax. They also worry about being in the middle of the long table, and hang around to bag the end seat. They do this to avoid the processing of energetic overwhelm, an unexplained feeling of crowding. They unconsciously prepare themselves for this, so will either experience an unexplained anxiety or will find themselves exhausted without knowing why.

Within this situation there's a perception of aggression, even when it's clear that none is present. The round table keeps everything equal – the hyper-vigilance calms down enough for the triggered earlier memories of a continued need to be vigilant to relax. The out-of-control monkey mind and unpredictability the Intuitive-Sensitive may have met earlier in their life has trained the wider, more broadly aware right hemisphere, to the extent that the internal instruction is: 'Best be prepared.'

Several times a year, following events I've hosted, I dine out in the company of my troop of fantastic helpers. Predictably enough, they are all Highly Intuitive-Sensitives, and usually at least 14 of us will head off to a restaurant. One particular place we go to in Dublin has become a standing joke. There's a speeding up as we reach the door, followed by a rush as everyone heads for the seats positioned facing the door; we all end up sitting in a row or squeezed in around the round table of the end. The restaurant's proprietor has become so used to this he is prepared for it. Everyone is happy, there are no awkward moments and people in the group who have never met each other before chat happily for hours.

This extra stimulation of the right hemisphere's broad vigilance, perhaps triggered by a disruptive early environment, is, I believe, the reason the intuitive component develops to a higher than average level. It's possibly therefore a survival mechanism of the right hemisphere, passed through the generations via epigenetic inheritance (DNA reaction to environmental situations passed through generations) or experienced first-hand.

This explains the Intuitive-Sensitive's drive for purpose; it's so strong because there's a forceful desire for freedom, an escape from a real or imagined imprisonment, an escape from containment. Purpose means freedom from the anxiety that we're somehow inherently stupid or even irrelevant in the world of the rational.

Purpose means freedom from aloneness in a world where we're surrounded by other people, in a world that's felt to us to be full of the need for control and restriction within a group of ideals set by the narrow focus of the left hemisphere.

Helena's story

Helena is a very Highly Intuitive-Sensitive, and since the beginning of her adult years, she's had a compulsion to keep moving. As a young adult she dreamed of moving always somewhere else, but she didn't know where. In her adult life, her marriage was happy but every three years she would wake up with a strong need to move home. Her husband would dutifully put the house on the market, ready for the next environment and the predictable next three years.

It wasn't until middle age that Helena realized why she had a need and a desire to keep moving. Prior to that, she would make a joke of her 'somewhere' lineage of gypsy roots to explain the origins of the constant compulsion to relocate. She realized that her background – growing up with a violent father – was one that she'd always made excuses for. She'd accepted the family's explanation for her father's behaviour – it was down to his 'artist's temper' and stress – and their assertion that he was a good, loyal provider. This kept her true belief – that the man was a cruelly calculating predator – at bay.

Throughout her adult life Helena had felt she needed to perform, but whatever her performance, it didn't feel good enough. Praise, she felt, had consequence attached to it; being noticed was dangerous. Moving gave her a new identity, a place she couldn't be seen.

It wasn't until Helena experienced the pain of one cruel comment too far from her father that she realized it was time to let go of being the perfect daughter. She finally decided to leave her father to it, and withdrew from his company altogether.

Years later, beyond the three-year mark in her current home, she was talking to her husband when the realization hit her. The ghost of the constant need to move on had been finally laid to rest. She realized the moving was about escaping a predatory feeling, the sense that something was coming after her, but she couldn't see what it was. She'd mistaken a feeling of purpose with a link to moving. She realized that she'd released herself from constantly attaining, or seeking to attain, the approval of her father. She'd finally seen that the approval was never going to come. But instead of that being a sorrowful loss, she had a feeling, probably for the first time in her life, of elation.

Having a sense of purpose in the world is so important to the Intuitive-Sensitive because it's outside the feeling of containment. The right hemisphere isn't dominant but it's the preferred way of being in the Intuitive. The right hemisphere understands life, the environment it's in, as a whole. It understands body language, metaphor, the seeing of things in context. It understands subtle meaning.

These are all traits of the Intuitive-Sensitive. It's about living life as life, rather than a series of mechanical expressions and meaning. The narrow focus of the left hemisphere likes tools and machines – not things we associate with purpose.

The chatty left-brain and the silent right-brain

Purpose is also about having a voice. McGilchrist mentions how the left hemisphere's view is fixed, isolated and static, while the right hemisphere's is fluid and open; again this is the general persona of the Intuitive-Sensitive. Intuition needs a flow, an openness and an ability to see outside the box.

Most important of all, perhaps, is that the right hemisphere has no voice, while the left is very vocal – it's literal, logical and processed. The left is loud in the inner world. Purpose gives the right hemisphere its voice; the internal view beyond the mundane, a feeling of connection, service and love.

The difference between humans and animals is the frontal lobe within the brain. This part of who we are gives us the capacity for empathy. It gives us the ability to step back. Intuitive-Sensitive People, in their purposeful flow, are able to step back; the left hemisphere makes life instant to the extent you're right there, up front, unable to see.

Step too far back, and you can't read the scenario. The connection comes from the emotions of the Intuitive-Sensitive, hence the reason they've often gone through a lot of emotional change in their life. They have, not only through their natural capability but also from their experiences, the ability to connect, to empathize with others.

The conflict lies within the left hemisphere's talk. This part is very convincing; it shuts out everything that doesn't fit with its model. It cuts us off, is very vocal in its beliefs and speaks on our behalf. The Intuitive-Sensitive finds it essential therefore to create purpose, to expand their world into their creative, expansive mind, to free themselves from a sense of internal restriction.

As Intuitive-Sensitives we often become tongue-tied and stressed around confrontation and a sense of containment. Purpose begins to create the autonomy we desire within our minds to free ourselves from the left hemisphere's drone of rules and apparent restrictions.

McGilchrist says we live in a world right now that has pursued perfection at the price of emptiness, within a closed box of what we know. We prioritize the virtual over the real, as technology becomes ever more important. A paradoxical relationship has formed between restraint and freedom as we pursue happiness, but it's leading to resentment and an explosion of depressive illness – which is fast becoming the world's number one health complaint.

Intuitive-Sensitives need purpose: they need it to experience who they are, an expression of a broader view. Containment, the rules of their own internal world and that of the outer universe, is too restrictive; it's contained within a narrow focus of 'This is what the truth is and you will believe it'. They want to burst out from that; they want to look into the mirror of what they know, and more of what they know is too much for their expanding inner world to cope with. At this stage there's always a conflict between what they want and what they think should be part of their world.

The Intuitive-Sensitive's natural capacity for empathy means their perception is *outerspection* rather than always introspection. They want to understand their capacity for shared emotional responses and seeing things through another's eyes. They feel labelled as overly jumpy, emotional – spooky, even – especially when they just 'know' about something. They want to nurture a possibility of life beyond such labels. Purpose gives them that access.

Today I watch my young sons with their own apparent internal conflict between the right- and left-hemisphere responses. My eldest son feels he loves the virtual world, the pretend expression through gaming with his friends over the internet. His closest friend has moved to Canada, and their virtual world is their meeting point. His focus is very narrow when playing: all is shut out while his world is closed further.

His Sensitive soul expression, though unimpressed with the containment, wants to see and experience a wider, broader view; his unconscious world is screaming already for this adjustment. He meets a young friend who lives locally – a girl. She likes a different world than that of dens, the forest and bike riding, and she's introduced his 'other side', one he didn't consciously know was there.

Now his pleasure is the balance of expansion, exploration and real expression. Even at 10 years old, he's discovering his immediate 'purpose'. He's realized he's at his happiest in his right-hemisphere world, while having a balance of his left more focused: interactions that his new friend is happy to accommodate.

> The Intuitive-Sensitive has the ability to help others see their wider view. Their purpose feels as though it's about helping others to see, to feel and to connect. However, the Intuitive-Sensitive has to learn that connection with others comes through connection with themselves.

Purpose comes through the quietened inner world, the connection to the whole picture and the courage to see it. But how do you get there? People ask me all the time how they can find what they're looking for – it feels just out of reach; no matter how much they stretch, it doesn't seem to come. This right- and left-hemisphere dynamic, the conflict around purpose, is something I see happening every day in the Intuitive-Sensitive; do they do what they feel is right, even if it appears unconventional, or do they go with what is known?

Often what is 'known' doesn't work for them; the conventional job that seemed like a good idea eats at something they can't explain. The cognitive therapy that works for everyone they know, but didn't work for them. The relationship that makes sense on paper – it's secure, sensible and everything's taken care of – but it just doesn't sit well. The Intuitive-Sensitive thinks it's their failure; it doesn't work for them and they think they should fit the accepted mould, however painful, and settle into what everyone around them seems to accept. The process is uncomfortable: they think it's them who's wrong, who's out of place.

They don't realize that their brain, their consciousness, is just asking them to see out through the eyes of their world and take in the wider view that others miss. This is why they need purpose: to feel it's worth seeking out. This is why faith is there, a deeper faith in what they're about, beyond what seems logical. And it's why their healing path is often different from what's always gone before.

An Intuitive-Sensitive's purpose, belonging and connection come through taking in the wider world – understanding individuals, not just the categories that everything is supposed to fit within. It's about learning. Living isn't a mechanical process, it's a feeling process. To understand that, healing has to take place outside the box of what's known and largely accepted.

Taking in an idea of consciousness beyond what's immediately known, what's experienced, often beyond what we can rationally explain, because at times there's no logical reasoning – it isn't a process we can box up and have the answer for. It just happens.

This is why I see Intuitive-Sensitives heal, moving much faster than those with a similar trauma towards resolving bitterness, anxiety, distrust and depression, because there's an engagement beyond a narrowly focused, conventional process. I've seen through years of engagement with such people that the process, the direct route, the beauty of what I least expected to happen, happens.

I'm immensely proud of these people because it takes trust, courage and faith to change convention, the established route to what is known. Even if it doesn't work for you, it takes courage, honesty and fortitude to face it. The transformations I've seen in people – their trust and faith in the larger, lesser-known picture, but *their* picture – has been an incredible process. I feel they have made a difference to their own little piece of humanity.

The 7 steps to deep insight

Through looking at my personal experiences and those of the thousands of Intuitive-Sensitives I've helped over the years, I've concluded that there are 7 steps that the Intuitive-Sensitive needs to take in order to feel that their intuition is helpful, and know that it can be used for a stronger sense of purpose, the personal place in which you feel the sense of emotional overwhelm dissolve.

These 7 steps have an order, but like all aspects of intuition, they don't necessarily proceed in that order. Some people have them operating all at the same time, others have more parts than others. The important thing to remember is that intuition isn't logical: it can't be boxed. It works in a fluid manner so it demands a fluid approach. In the next section I've put the seven steps in an order, but do bear in mind they can move within this, depending on the person and their individual life experience.

The 7 steps will take you through your own personal journey, a place of expansion, while reconciling the wayward aspects of the monkey mind. The steps move through accepting your Sensitive difference into quietening the mind, hearing the 'soul', the relevance of power struggles, how to access your super-intuitive state, why courage is necessary for self-realization and finally, the powerful experience of uniting the inner child and the adult self.

In Part II I'm going to share with you the 7 steps of the flourishing Intuitive process. This is your story going forward....

Part II

The 7 Steps to Purpose: Learn to Enhance Your Intuitive Skills

Chapter 7

Step 1: Accept Your Difference

'There's something wrong with me – I'm overly sensitive to people. At work, sometimes I'm on the verge of tears when I'm expressing something important to me. It's making me exhausted, and I don't want to feel other people's feelings any more. What can I do about it?'

The first step to utilizing your intuitive skills is to realize that there's nothing wrong with you. It's about accepting that you're different, not broken. There's nothing to fix, only things to discover. And there are others exactly like you.

However, during the early days of discovering your intuitive insight you may often feel alone in your immediate environment; you may feel misunderstood and sometimes devastated by the fact that you feel and see things that others haven't the perception to notice. My first steps into the world of intuitive insight weren't something I wanted. Like most Intuitive-Sensitives I didn't wake up one morning and decide to have a unique insight into others' lives or an uncanny connection to aspects of people's future behaviour or actions. It was something that happened to me – I didn't ask for it.

Long before I could identify what was happening, I knew about other people's lives, often expressing what I thought they'd told me, although they hadn't. On one occasion I got into deep trouble after telling friends about a mutual friend's pregnancy. I told everyone, apparently, that she was pregnant with a boy.

I believed my friend had told me the news herself – I was convinced of it. 'I'm pregnant Heidi – but you've ruined my surprise,' she complained. 'I don't know if it's a boy. I haven't told a soul I'm pregnant but you seem to have.' I apologized profusely, incredibly confused as to how it had happened. She did indeed go on to have a boy.

> Many Intuitive-Sensitives go through a period of spontaneously revealing secrets they didn't mean to. These are always events they've not been told about but seem to know. These communications are not hocus-pocus; they're revealed to the conscious mind from unconscious thought fields.

Many of these instances occur away from seeing or hearing a person, and they don't involve trickery, reading body language or distinguishing someone's tone of voice. In the case of my friend and her pregnancy, it turned out that I hadn't actually seen or spoken to her prior to my telling others she was pregnant.

I receive emails on a weekly basis from those to whom I've revealed a part of their lives. The information comes in metaphors, examples through pictured symbolism in my mind – it makes no sense to me but an enormous amount of sense to them. These are just some of the ways my intuition is presented. I'm not unique within the experiences of Intuitive-Sensitives – it happens to us constantly, and much of it isn't asked for.

As I explained earlier, I do believe, from my own experiences and those of the thousands of Intuitive-Sensitives I've helped over the years, there are aspects of a person's early experiences that give them a predisposition to their natural insight. I also believe that some of those aspects are housed within the neurological viewpoint of consciousness originating within the brain; I've witnessed others as an aspect of consciousness independent of our own abilities.

The cleverness of the unconscious, and how it communicates with our everyday awareness, is too masterful for it simply to be a brain mechanism. There has to be a form of intelligence outside it. Naturally developing Intuitive-Sensitive People provide a link to this; their task is to interpret what's presented. The brain will, of course, present the information as it has done through the centuries: through symbolism rather than in a literal form.

Why a stranger will tell you their life story

The early developmental stage of the intuitive opening process is incredibly confusing and uncomfortable for the Intuitive-Sensitive Person. It's presented in the mind – often as a re-run of something you saw earlier, even months or years earlier. For example, you're sitting on a train, reading a book, when a person sits down next to you. Suddenly your mind's overtaken by a vivid replay of a scene in a TV drama you watched a few months ago; the scene involved a big argument.

If you then struck up a conversation with the person sitting next to you, you'd discover why your peaceful thoughts had been invaded in this way. You'd find that they have arguments going on in their life, which they're trying to resolve. The stronger the scene that's shown in your mind, the stronger their feelings will be around this argument. And if you chose not to speak to the person, you'd still have had a significant (and unwanted) view of their personal thoughts.

These kinds of experience feel invasive, scary and deeply unsettling, until you have a decent understanding of what's happening, why, and how to solve it. The first step is to realize that your intuitive skills are not some unsightly curse to be erased – or a party trick. They're a normal part of your particular workings – a more aware right-hemisphere taking in its surroundings, and a triggered emotional response to try to be of help and assistance (empathy) for a person's dilemma.

This is why when you have these intuitive instincts as part of your foundational make-up, every stranger in the land wants to tell you their life story. They express to you the parts they've never told another soul, leaving you wondering what you have stamped on your head that attracts it!

Why intuitive insight doesn't work in a laboratory

One of the things most Intuitive-Sensitive People worry about is how they're seen in the outer world. In acknowledging that weird things happen to them with regard to other people, their thoughts, emotions and life events, they're concerned it'll marginalize them, or worse, lead them to the nearest mental health facility.

When you put an Intuitive-Sensitive Person on the spot you tie them to certain outcomes, and as a result they become frightened; they feel cornered and trapped. As soon as this happens, the fluidity of their intuitive input shuts down.

Within our own circuits of brain function, when we feel cornered we look for hard and fast facts. These are more effectively organized in our left-hemisphere. The left-brain will start its very convincing talk – it'll shut out everything that doesn't fit with its model, cutting it off. The defensive self kicks in, a protective action that makes it easy for us to narrow our focus and more tricky to open to the expansive view. We then operate within what we know.

Intuitive people aren't immune to what I call a 'left-hemisphere takeover'. This is the state within ourselves in which a balance of the two worlds of our internal process doesn't happen. It becomes locked in fear: one-sided and narrow in focus. We can't see a way forward and feel trapped; we have a compulsion to follow what we already know, even if it's desperately uncomfortable.

When a left-hemisphere takeover happens there's no chance we can operate within our intuitive focus. This is because we're scared, petrified even, of getting it wrong. The left-hemisphere has given us a close, up-front view – and with it an inability to step back, to see the wider picture.

In science, experiments take place within a controlled environment, and proof is ascertained by repeating an experiment and gaining the same results over and over again. The materialist philosopher Paul Churchland says that: '... there's not a single parapsychological effect that can be repeatedly or reliably produced in any laboratory suitably equipped to perform and control the experiment. Not one.'

This isn't surprising! Intuition doesn't adjust to the requirements of left-hemisphere organization – it can't become a narrow focus because it's instant, in the moment, and it'll disappear as quickly as you try to contain it.

> The mistake is in trying to make the intuitive process tangible – to control it, to see it as some kind of enemy to be contained, locked down, broken up into explainable bits – rather than seeing it as a connection to a poetic beauty, process and clear insight.

This is why it's so important for an Intuitive-Sensitive Person to *accept* their insights, their sensitivity, as the way they are built. Otherwise they become the nervous wreck hostage of a left-hemisphere takeover, trying to fit the narrow moulds presented to them as the 'truth'.

How to avoid a 'left-hemisphere takeover'

People sometimes wonder why others don't remove themselves from uncomfortable situations – stop eating junk when they are morbidly obese, say, or leave an abusive partner. If it were easy, people would make the change. The reason they don't, from what I've seen, is that they're in the grip of a left-hemisphere takeover.

You know you're in the grip of a left-hemisphere takeover when people in your external world judge you for your intuitive perspective, or you believe they will. In the early days of acknowledging my own intuitive insight, I was heavily judged. I felt punished for questioning a framework I thought I was meant to fit into. It wasn't until I realized that true judgement came from within that I saw that others were reflecting a part of me. They were reflecting back the part of my inner world that judged, that critically questioned me.

In this sphere I felt contained, trapped and miserable within a world that reflected back more of what I knew than what I wanted to know. I craved expansion, yet I couldn't have it, not until I'd weaved a path to my own inner acceptance – a truce, for want of a better expression, between the left- and right-hemispheres.

Although a left-hemisphere takeover is symbolic, for the Intuitive-Sensitive its effects are far from so. Our internal world becomes paralyzed, frustrating and immovable. When others suggest we try a moment of 'positive thinking' it annoys us intensely. If we could have that moment we would, especially when we're well and truly on the road to self-awareness. Conscious positive thinking is the norm. When we're in a left-hemisphere lock-down, though, there's no chance. This frame of mind isn't the place to judge our own actions, it's about having compassion for them.

To find your way out of a left-hemisphere takeover, it's essential to take a moment to try to prevent the one-sided internal lockdown. How will you know it's coming? In my experience, a left-hemisphere lockdown is always preceded by a growing feeling of irritability: a desire to get into your own space. For some, the feelings of overwhelm become strong; others experience a rising numbness before wanting to withdraw. There's guilt attached to the withdrawal, so a feeling of shame begins to rise, too, then an over-compensation in order to feel there's still approval from others.

Antony's story

Anthony is in the process of deepening his spiritual understanding. He's very intuitive and is in the throes of accepting his Intuitive-Sensitivity, which also means understanding when he's shutting parts of himself out. He's going through an internal crisis of confidence in which there's considerable self-rejection. Now in the grip of a strong left-hemisphere takeover, he's overwhelmed by irritation.

Anthony's early life was characterized by disruption and his parents were emotionally abusive. His intuitive capabilities grew strongly during his formative years, and he's now trying to accept the gentle nature, kindness and sense of humour that others can see in him but he can't see in himself. As his sensitivity becomes part of his world, he feels he should reject it, as it doesn't fit with his family's roots.

Anthony isn't used to people noticing him; he notices things for everyone else. He's very keen to use his intuitive capabilities to help others, but at this stage, before he can go further with it, he needs to become comfortable with his own instincts. On a regular basis I ask Anthony to send me his thoughts on how he's been feeling in the previous week. I ask him what he's been eating, what he's been doing and what he thinks about the world right now. I ask him these things to help him to train himself out of shutting himself down at the point of his opening up.

Anthony now needs to make the transition away from the perception of himself he's been trained to believe, which includes the idea that he's a lesser being. Anthony is far from weak; in fact he's one of the strongest, most determined people I've met. That move across in his internal world will need to come with a wider expansive thinking, an acknowledgement of his value in the world. At some deep level he believes this to be a fanciful and unjustified position, and this isn't uncommon during the acceptance stage.

The people in Anthony's life don't notice that he's been on the receiving end of abusive behaviour. Why? Some people are numb to this, or distract themselves from the realization that certain behaviours are inherently wrong, that they hurt and they cause harm. Intuitive-Sensitive People, through their strongly empathetic nature, can feel it's not right, even if their own heritage is covered in abuse and they know nothing else. Sometimes the tricky bit is making the internal step across; it feels as though you're being disloyal to something, even if that doesn't logically make sense.

Anthony battles with his keyboard every week. He sends me something about his world and what's going on in it right now. I laughed out loud recently when I read his latest account: 'Heidi, the world and all that's in it can F-off quite frankly.' I thought, great progress – he's being honest. He'll soon make the shift over.

––––––

The moral of this story, though, is that when you feel a narrowing of the mind coming on, when you feel at war with the world, try to view it as a left-hemisphere takeover: it's a part of you trying to protect you, fold you into what you know of the world, to keep you restricted and out of what it feels is too new and unexplored. It's a ploy to keep you bound in the safety of what it knows.

When you're in the process of accepting your intuitive senses and your sensitivity, it's about realizing that the more self-judgements you make, the deeper the perceived block to and rejection of your natural senses opening up.

On a daily basis I see people who are terrified that their intuitive perceptions and way of connecting with the world are somehow going to be found out and that they'll therefore be humiliated. Their left-hemisphere takeover is their attempt to fit in to more of the world that they believe to be everyone else's understanding; they have a deep fear that their own world is somehow hideously abnormal.

Accepting your Intuitive-Sensitivity

The words of the British philosopher Bertrand Russell sum up how a truly Intuitive-Sensitive Person looks out: 'The whole problem with the world is that fools and fanatics are always so certain of themselves, and wiser people so full of doubts.' In all of the audiences I've spoken to, I've never yet seen a genuine Intuitive-Sensitive Person who is particularly forthcoming about their abilities.

The question I'm always asked is: 'How do I know if my intuition is genuine and not part of an overactive imagination? I'm afraid to use it in case I ever get it wrong.' My answer is that I would be worried if they *didn't* worry about getting it wrong! Worrying makes you more inclined to make sure you view what you see or sense from a place of high integrity – always concerned about how others perceive what you might be offering as a way of seeing something in life moving forwards.

Intuitive-Sensitivity is without doubt a responsibility, one that wasn't chosen or asked for by those who possess it. This, though, doesn't take away the fact that most Intuitive-Sensitives have an incredible desire and capacity for kindness, something that's very much linked to their 'right-brain' nature. Part of this characteristic often means they are the least narcissistic people you can come across.

They worry about being narcissistic, and that worry alone makes them the least likely to be so. You don't have to look far within them to see that anything they are good at is very quickly dismissed as unimportant. They struggle to admit that anything they have a talent for is important.

They lie awake at night, worried they are going to be found out: that someone will recognize them as the 'impostor' they are. The truth will be discovered, they think: they should never have been trusted, they're not supposed to be in the position they're in. They want people to be respectful, but find it hard to accept that people *do* respect what they offer.

Intuitive-Sensitives and Imposter Syndrome

This may all sound like the crazy thoughts of a paranoid person, rather than the normal thoughts of a kind, gentle individual who has others' best interests always as their own interests. The truth is, most Intuitive-Sensitive People suffer from what's known as Impostor Syndrome – the sense that someday they'll be 'found out'.

They have a persistent belief that they lack intelligence, despite a lot of evidence to the contrary. Success for them is more a feeling of relief than joy, and other people's praise and recognition for their accomplishments are undeserved – they feel that their achievements are a result of chance, charm, connections or some other external factor.

The term Impostor Syndrome was first introduced in a 1978 paper by psychologists Pauline Clance and Suzanne Imes called 'The Impostor Phenomenon in High Achieving Women'. In it they revealed that many of their high-achieving students admitted during counselling they felt their success was undeserved. Today the term is used to refer to an inability to internalize or feel deserving of your success.

> In an Intuitive-Sensitive Person, Impostor Syndrome is an endearing trait and a positive issue – despite the mind-bending attacks of anxiety and self-doubt it causes – for it helps them remain in their open-ended kindness and empathetic nature.

However, I believe there are two parts to the darker side of the syndrome, and it's necessary for the Intuitive-Sensitive Person to heal these as part of their progress. Impostor Syndrome leaves a space – a big hole that will be filled in life. If it's not acknowledged, the hole will either fill with procrastination or it'll meet the world of the predator. We'll look at the latter in a moment, but first, it's important to understand where that feeling that you're a fraud originates.

Impostor feelings can spawn from subtle early life messages. For example, in school, if you generally achieved A grades and then received a B, your parents' focus might have been on the B not being an A. This focus can create a child who grows up to become a perfectionist. Or you may have been raised in a family where your talents went unnoticed, your accomplishments ignored or barely acknowledged.

When I see Imposter Syndrome occurring in an Intuitive-Sensitive Person's life, it's usually the case that they grew up with a close member of the family who was a pathological narcissist. This made their life whole-heartedly about pacifying the narcissist, making sure they were number one and that everybody knew it. As a background, this also substantially contributes to any 'people-pleasing' tendencies.

Alternatively it can simply be that in your early life, your parents didn't want to single you out for praise, in case it upset one of your siblings. Whatever the reason, Impostor Syndrome can lead the adult years to become about dumbing down and not feeling your accomplishments. This diminishing of what you've achieved can have, in some instances, catastrophic consequences. This shortfall in self-worth, to the level that you're not appreciating who you are, leaves big gaps in your boundaries around your intuitive skills. These gaps make it easy for the predator to become part of your life.

The role of the sociopathic predator

Several years ago, I came across a book I was strongly attracted to, yet very afraid to pick up. I kept it on a shelf for a long while before opening it. The book was Martha Stout's *The Sociopath Next Door*. Since it's publication there have been numerous popular texts on the subject of psychopaths, or in American terms, sociopaths. Understanding this area is crucial as a first step to accepting your intuitive process. Why? Because sociopaths are very attracted to Sensitive, empathetic people.

> It's estimated that one in 25 people are on the sociopathic scale. And the higher your propensity for Impostor Syndrome, the higher your chances of having a direct experience with a sociopath: they will use it as a way in.

Sociopaths hide in plain sight in life. They are people without a conscience. Although they are generally not mass murderers, aggressive criminals or blatant law-breakers, they are life's ruthless snipers. They are manipulative and socially cruel, and with a charming persona – 'butter wouldn't melt' in their 'innocent' mouths.

In psychiatry, sociopaths are defined as having Anti-Social Behavioural Disorder, and there are numerous references to childhood or teenage delinquency. The book and movie *We Need to Talk About Kevin* give a very clear picture of what a teenage sociopath with a highly aggressive aspect looks like. Generally though, sociopaths operate surreptitiously, hidden among society.

The traits of a sociopath

Sociopaths are defined in several ways, but generally they display at least three of the following traits, which they use to often devastating effect on the Intuitive-Sensitive People they come into contact with:

∽ A failure to conform to social norms. Sociopaths don't like to follow the rules. To them, rules are fun to break, and guidelines are to be ignored. To the Intuitive-Sensitive, this trait is uncomfortable; the sociopath will mock the Intuitive's desire to stay within the rules, while they blatantly break them.

∽ Deceitfulness and manipulation. Sociopaths are incredibly manipulative and don't think twice about lying. Their level of manipulation is so extreme that it shocks the Intuitive-Sensitive, who finds it inconceivable that such behaviour is humanly possible. The sociopath will find this amusing; they'll utilize the Intuitive's fear to the level of consistent humiliation, jokes and minimizing. This sends the Intuitive off course and they therefore become easy to manipulate, despite their levels of intuition in other situations.

∽ Impulsiveness and a failure to plan ahead. Sociopaths are 'in the moment' people. Initially they appear to be charming and fun to be around, their spontaneity momentarily engaging. The truth is, they need constant stimulation, so they'll be very adept at creating instant drama. To the Intuitive-Sensitive this is intensely over-stimulating and if they've been around a sociopath in early life this will be one of the reasons for their hyper-vigilance in adulthood.

~ Irritability and aggression. Being around a sociopath means you'll very quickly be 'walking on eggshells'. Their aggression and irritability are instantaneous, and the reason for them is known only to them. They'll never apologize for it, and the Intuitive-Sensitive will either feel responsible for the sociopath's behaviour or they'll feel intensely sorry for them. Sociopaths love to feed off a 'sob story': they'll often have a great one lined up. It will be lies with an element of truth, to make it plausible.

~ A reckless disregard for the safety of themselves and others. A sociopath will take what are often ludicrous risks, with a glint in their eye. To the Intuitive-Sensitive there's a lurch in the stomach; they're supposed to keep up, somehow, yet their body screams 'no'. Sociopaths are adrenaline junkies, taking pleasure in dangerous things, activities or behaviours.

~ A consistent irresponsibility. Nothing is ever their fault: in fact it's your fault. Every wrongdoing they engage in is directed back to you. If you ever get something that resembles an apology, it will go no further than, 'I'm sorry you feel that way'; it will never be, 'I'm sorry for making you feel that way.'

~ A lack of remorse after hurting someone. An Intuitive-Sensitive, due to their very high levels of empathy, will often spend days, weeks, months, even years, worrying about something they said or did to someone that upset them. A sociopath will never worry or even feel they did something wrong. They will, however, use the guilt that an Intuitive Person feels, even when they're not guilty of any misdemeanour.

There are other components associated with the sociopathic personality, such as the part that draws most people in: the glib, superficial charm, a glow of charisma that makes them seem more interesting. They are more spontaneous, more complex, than everyone else. This is something the rescuer part of the Sensitive-Intuitive finds very appealing – it's something to take care of, to help fix. Sociopaths have a narcissistic personality, a huge sense of self-importance that the Intuitive Person with Impostor Syndrome finds especially attractive.

The sociopath in the Intuitive-Sensitive's life

I've seen many an Intuitive-Sensitive's life – in the early stages of their development – destroyed by a sociopathic partner, parent, sibling, boss or co-worker, their inner world mutilated by the humiliating head games the sociopath plays. The instant switch to a charming 'Who, me?' smile when questioned. Other people will say, 'No, I don't believe you, he/she's so good looking, they can't be that bad.'

The sociopath will have deliberately targeted the Intuitive-Sensitive because they look for caring, empathetic people. They hit on them with their sob story. The Intuitive-Sensitive will want to be of help or assistance – they'll seek to 'save' the person from their plight. Sociopaths target empathetic people who have a strong need to feel loved. They'll fill the missing hole by becoming the ideal.

If you've experienced this, before you feel you've become some kind of failure for allowing a sociopath to find their way into your life, it's necessary to know that they prepare for their engagement with you. First of all they will learn everything about you. As predatory manipulators, they'll become the person missing from your life.

For example, if you grew up without a father, they'll become a surrogate dad. If you've been abandoned in life, they'll be there for you – the fully engaged person who'll never let you down, even if you've only known them for five minutes. They'll create a chemical bond that masquerades as true connection, a 'soulmate' even. They do this through 'love bombing' and flattery to the point of chemical saturation. With your body full of the 'love chemicals', rather than intuition, you'll think this is the best person ever to have engaged in your life.

It won't be long though before the true aspects of their nature come forward. Although they have no capacity for empathy or conscience, they will use that of the Intuitive-Sensitive to give the impression they care about life, love and people. Highly empathetic people often find themselves as the mouthpiece for sociopaths: they'll use the empathetic person's capacity for loyalty, kindness and social connectivity as their playpen. This is why an Intuitive-Sensitive is so devastated when they realize they have been hoodwinked by a sociopath.

This internal devastation leads to a collapse of self-faith, a mortifying belief they're worth less than nothing, especially as the sociopath isn't in the least bit interested in their welfare. They move on, just like that, without a care in the world or a backward glance.

> I've seen how some Intuitive-Sensitives become obsessed for years, trying to re-engage the interest of the sociopath; they can't believe they've been so carelessly shoved to one side, a meaningless part of their business.

Often when I'm asked to have a look at the energy of someone who's troubling an Intuitive-Sensitive I often come across what

I so readily recognize: sociopathic energy feels energetically as a void, an empty space without personality. It doesn't feel to me as though it has an inner world. When they are active with something that's of interest to them, the sociopath will see any trouble they are causing as fun – that of an opponent rather than a person. The 'opponent' to them is often something that should squirm in pain; they have a spooky level of enjoyment in watching someone suffer.

Simon's story

Recently I helped a man called Simon who worked in the City of London in a financial institution. He was owed millions by a man who he felt was his friend. He described this friend as a good guy with whom he'd worked on several projects. Simon had helped build a facility for his friend's company and it had gone on to make him hundreds of millions in financial revenue, and Simon was owed five million of it.

The guy – we'll call him Steve – was full of promises: he was going to pay Simon what he was due. Simon asked me what I felt intuitively to be the situation, as he now really needed to collect his payment: he'd been waiting two years for it. As soon as I looked at Steve's energy, I was immediately taken over by the feeling of emptiness, a game being played. I told Simon that Steve had no intention of paying him, not until the last minute of truly having to, and even then he'd be lucky. I told Simon if he wanted to receive his money he'd have to start accepting that Steve was a sociopath, and play it that way.

To cut a long story short, Simon went abroad on a business trip for Steve, as he still wanted to give his 'friend' the benefit of the doubt. Not a penny had been paid, and Simon, now financially desperate, spoke to Steve, who gave him a strong 'we're buddies' story: 'You should have asked,' he added. 'I would have paid you a million already.' The next day Steve denied all knowledge of their conversation, and cut Simon off altogether.

By this time, Simon's emotions, his health, his belief in himself, and his status in the City were in tatters, and he was desperate to listen when he again contacted me. I told him exactly what I felt he should do. It would take him a month to do it, but if he followed exactly what I felt was the way, he would get his money. It wasn't about some mysterious process; it was simply down to the fact that I've had a lot of experience of looking into the processes of the sociopath's mind, to the extent that I'm aware of what motivates them. And then I looked into the Intuitive process of how to solve it.

Simon was very frightened to do what I'd told him, although it was nothing elaborate – simply a few strategic moves that involved him disappearing off the radar, preventing Steve from getting hold of him for a month or two. Simon followed this procedure exactly, which I know was really hard for him to do because he's an honest man who likes honest communication and looks for a way to work things out. These were all aspects of Simon's character that Steve had been using wildly to his advantage.

Within three days of Simon becoming visible to Steve once again, the money was paid into his bank account. Why? Simon didn't have to threaten Steve and he didn't have to confront him: he simply needed to engage what he already knew deep inside about Steve from the outset, but didn't want to believe.

For two years Simon's life had been taken over by a sociopath. Their relationship had cost him his romantic relationship, his home, his self-esteem and his reputation. Steve was typical in his sociopathic behaviour, making sure he rubbished Simon the moment he felt he was on the verge of refusing to participate in anything that didn't seem 100 per cent above board.

It was now time to get out, once and for all, without Simon having to say a word about it. Steve knew he'd been found out, and that his safest option was to cut Simon loose. And he did this by finally paying him, something no sociopath likes to do.

But why do Intuitive-Sensitive People attract such predators? What's the purpose? It's the process of angels and demons. This polarity has been present throughout history. It's seen in mythology: the hero has always explored the underworld, found himself in darkness before reaching the light.

Whether this is true or not, it's an interesting theory and one I know that Intuitive-Sensitives do benefit from eventually. The sociopathic temperament is an evolutionary offshoot of the human race, their consciousness is activated and driven to attack the rest of us. But why would this happen?

It's to help us to develop a more intuitive, compassionate lifestyle. The predator's behaviour helps us to realize the beauty of human empathy and connection – the basis of human development. In essence, sociopaths teach us that kindness isn't to be taken for granted. They painfully stop us from becoming complacent.

Summary and action ideas

∿ Intuitive-Sensitivity isn't something that's asked for: the people who have it didn't wake up one day and decide to be intuitive, to know about another's life or aspects of their own. It just happened to them, and for some it's a frighteningly unwanted experience that won't go away.

∿ The first step to realizing your intuitive capabilities, and to utilize them for good, is to accept that your gentle, compassionate nature isn't naïve stupidity or an overly sensitive wound you hide from the world.

∿ Hiding your Intuitive-Sensitivity leads to a deeper issue in the shape of Impostor Syndrome: a fear most Intuitive-Sensitives have. But it's a healthy fear in the sense that it keeps us aware of other people; it keeps the intuitive senses questioned and therefore safely out of the realms of ego-based opinion.

∿ Rejecting our intuitive self – trying to keep it hidden away – contributes to a 'left-hemisphere takeover': a narrowing of our perceptions that leads us to feel scared of getting it wrong. This gives us an up-front, immediate view of the world, instead of the wider, more relaxed focus required for intuitive focus. Moving beyond a 'left-hemisphere takeover' means accepting our Sensitive, intuitive nature.

∿ Left-hemisphere takeovers and Impostor Syndrome can make Intuitive-Sensitives very accessible to members of society with a predatory temperament: those who have sociopathic characteristics.

∿ Sustained and active development of your intuitive senses helps to build the skill of noticing the predator, learning where they are in life, and eventually, how to negotiate them without having to engage with what they feed off – confrontation.

~ The main purpose of having to work through the darkness of shadowy characters is to find your own light. Such encounters help you to truly understand others, and to develop your own reliable radar for those with an absence of conscience. This is the process of beginning to trust your first impressions, the truth of your natural intuition.

Chapter 8

Step 2: Learn to Manage Your Mind

'Never be ashamed of a scar, it simply means you were stronger than whatever tried to hurt you.'
UNKNOWN

The Intuitive-Sensitive Person's dream is an inner world of calm communication. It's a world that doesn't lie; it doesn't over-stimulate your senses or send you into panic at the thought of confrontation; and it doesn't assume the worst at every turn. The Intuitive-Sensitive individuals in this world would like to live their life in a state of sustainable, enlightened peace.

All of this sounds unrealistic and far removed from the real world with its normal challenges, but the fact is that it *is* possible. An inner world of calm, collected peace as the majority experience of your thoughts and feelings, while still engaging your intuitive process, is more than realistic. The trouble is, it takes courage to get there.

Rebuilding the 'broken vase'

'This experience in my life – the constant onslaught on my emotions, the exhaustion in my body, and on my wellbeing – has created a feeling I can only describe as like a broken vase. It's smashed into a million pieces and I don't know how to fix it.'

These were my feelings, and I know the challenge starts in the same way for many other Intuitive-Sensitive People. I've had more than my fair share of tough experiences, the majority of which have pushed me on to a deeper understanding and the ability to connect with other people. The challenges have given me a realistic insight into how events really impact people. Getting over it, and pulling yourself together, is easier said than done.

The key thing I've seen and experienced is understanding and pursuing the journey to one of the greatest gifts of all, mind management.

> Mind management isn't mind-over-matter or getting a grip, it's a deeper journey that involves the most empathetic part of our nature – viewing the inner world from a place of humanity, rather than castigation.

I started the process of mind management through admitting to myself that the inner vase, the porcelain piece we all spend our lives trying to protect, was smashed to tiny pieces. I had nothing left to give, no inner resources to call upon, nothing.

I decided to take each broken piece of the vase and start rebuilding it, and mind management was part of the journey. As each piece is placed back together, glued and crafted, a whole new pattern emerges: the missing pieces or those too small to glue, replaced by clear or coloured glass. The vase will always be imperfect – the pattern gives it away, and it's clear that it was once damaged – but it catches the light and sparkles in a different way to the once pure, porcelain piece.

My journey through life has been about helping others notice when their vase is smashed and needs rebuilding. They find themselves asking me how to, essentially, repair their vase. Rather than scream that it's broken and wish for someone else to fix it from the outer world, or a relationship or a different job to solve it, it's a process of building from the inside out. I know deep inside if my vase is smashed again, I can repair it. I will use more resources to repair it. I've gained a deeper faith in humanity and connection, despite many challenging circumstances. This faith isn't in anything external, the process is internal, the glue that sticks – my intuitive process.

I vividly remember my vase crumbling from the inside on two occasions. This was a process I could do nothing to solve. It felt like the approach of a giant wave, something I knew would swamp and drown me. On both occasions I felt the wave coming before it was supposed to. It isn't unusual for Intuitive-Sensitive People to have this sensation; many of us will feel a disruption in the body often years before it shows medically.

My giant wave was a taboo subject that many mothers never speak of. I know from my own experience, and from others who have had it, that speaking of the terror of pre- and postnatal illness is something you spend your life trying to avoid. The pain is overwhelming, the turmoil beyond words, and the impact when it hits, horrific. It's an illness way beyond baby blues, 'normal' depression or a fear of motherhood.

Every woman I've spoken to who has had the illness has never spoken of the full impact. It's a war wound you silently share, through the glassy-eyed stare of knowing. The first time I had severe postnatal depression was around the birth of my first son. That part of my emotional life is a blur; I've little to no recollection of the first two years of his life. This experience of the vase smashing, the pieces popping, was not the first time the vase had been broken.

I had at the time huge amounts of exposure to meditation, inner development and intuitive experience. None of these stopped the process from happening; they did, though, make it easier for me to understand it.

As the wave descended I could recognize what it was immediately, and I chose in that moment to observe the experience rather than absorb it. How could I do this? I had begun the active process of mind management: an active, honest inner communication.

As I felt the wave, instead of rejecting it, I accepted it was part of my process. I immediately informed the health professionals around me: a duty I felt to both my child and my husband. Many women with the illness cannot recognize it when it arrives and it takes someone else to see it; or they ignore it until the situation is evidently critical.

For the first two years of my eldest son's life I silently rebuilt the vase, piece by piece. Few people around me would have known I was ill. There was some evidence of it on the outside, as my immune system, under pressure, also began to bulge.

When I summed up the courage seven years later to have another child, I knew there would be a risk. I hadn't bargained for the risk I did experience at birth, but I distinctly remember feeling the same wave coming, between seven and eight months into my pregnancy. This time, with my knowledge and mind management much stronger, I surrendered to the vase popping, as the process was repeated.

This time though, because I knew the level of self-awareness I had and the work I had done, the experience was not a self-inflicted misery. It wasn't something to wallow in – 'not being good enough,' a failure as a mother – even though it was tempting, especially given the work I do.

My postnatal experiences will most certainly have had an impact on my two sons. They will have created another generation of highly, if not hyper-sensitive, individuals. Their sensory output is already extremely strong. My youngest son covers his eyes at the sight of anything emotional on the television; he even covers them for Barbie's interaction with the 'Bad fairy'.

My eldest is a stickler for fair behaviour and calmness, and he avoids the heavily action-orientated movies favoured by his peers. Both are deeply stressed by and can see immediately any form of aggression in other people. They are both very loyal, quick to speak up if they see an injustice directed at another and neither like rough games or contact sports.

It's my view that my sons already feel more sharply than their peers. This is something that will always be part of their lives, whether I created that through my conscious but still deeply impactful postnatal experiences, or whether it was already developed in the womb.

My reason for sharing these experiences is to bring to the fore the idea that there's no point in wishing your sensitivity away or trying to ignore it. A life focused on trying to protect your vase from being smashed is fruitless, limiting and frustrating. You'll still make mistakes in life, as I have. It's about being brave enough to trust yourself each time your vase is damaged and knowing you have the resources to rebuild it.

That knowing is mind management, and the resource is your willingness to use your intuitive progress.

Preparing for successful mind management

Part of developing our intuition, and certainly part of the journey to mind management, is the process of realizing that the vase exists – locked away in a secret room, deep inside the recesses of your unconscious inner world. It's one I believe we all pass through.

That process is much like what Elisabeth Kübler-Ross describes, in her 1969 book *On Death and Dying*, as the five stages of grief. For Intuitive-Senstivites though, Kübler-Ross's denial, anger, bargaining, depression and acceptance become: *resistance, denial, frustration, rejection, and trust.*

Resistance

Over the years I've hosted many development groups for Intuitive-Sensitives, and some of those have been made up of the same people for a period of four years. In those groups particularly, I observed a very similar journey within the attendees, regardless of their background. There was a strong inner resistance to becoming part of the group. A large number of the people really wanted to be there, but a few had tried everything possible to avoid attending.

I find that this still happens within the groups that attend my day workshops. I hear of sat navs turning to Mandarin and randomly re-routing people, or a searing resistance when attendees come to leave the house. Nonetheless, they manage to get there. This resistance pounds aggressively within the inner workings, a feeling that something is about to change, over which there's no control.

Resistance was a central component of Freud's psychoanalytic theory. He believed the process of bringing the unconscious to light is associated with pain, and because of the pain, the person will seek to reject it; therefore he will seek to keep things remaining the same, in order to avoid the experience of psychological pain.

Denial

Based on what I've seen, I agree with Freud's theory. This is where the second component, denial, comes into the equation. I've seen Intuitive-Sensitives cling desperately to what they know, even though it's not what they want. A part of them is so keen to let go, especially when a part of the unconscious has started to reveal itself, but this other part snaps in there, doing its job to keep the status quo.

The 'yes but, no but' excuses pour forth from their mouths; we're all guilty of it. For many, this will show in the form of co-dependent relationships – connections made through fear of loss rather than a true experience of love.

The journey to mind management is unattainable unless pain is felt with the beginning of an honest acknowledgement of what has hurt – what has wounded or overwhelmed – our Sensitive nature.

The nervous system is hard-wired to experience pain at high-definition levels; pain is therefore not the Intuitive-Sensitive Person's idea of fun. Yet without locating emotional pain, it's difficult to progress our intuitive insight to a higher level. Without being able to feel deeply, we can't interpret our intuition properly.

Recently, while I was hosting a seminar, a question came up from an attendee about her young son, who had experienced a complete breakdown after having suffered extreme bullying, and had been admitted to a medium secure mental health unit. He'd been in this environment for a year with little to no progress. The woman was due to visit her son on the Monday, and the day she spoke about this was Saturday.

A stunned silence fell as the woman told her story. To a room full of Intuitive-Sensitives, her pain for her son was *their* pain; some began to cry as she recalled her son's journey, her frustration at how nothing was moving coupled with the bureaucratic resistance she was up against.

I asked the group to hold in their minds a feeling of openness – no matter how much their own world wanted to interfere or judge the injustice they felt for this young man's situation. I asked them to hold it for long enough for me to intuitively 'feel' my way into his world, his unconscious thoughts and his feelings.

While in there, I expressed how I felt he felt. His awareness spoke of being desperate to go outside, although he wasn't allowed to. He didn't know how to express what the doctors wanted him to express; it came out 'all wrong'. His consciousness spoke of his deep terror – a terror he couldn't find any words to communicate.

For a period of 10 minutes or so, the whole room felt a deep compassion for this young man's pain. We let pain, normally an experience we do our best to avoid, flood through our consciousness in an expression of total empathy. When the experience felt complete, I thanked the audience for their assistance and repeated how I felt that the young man had somehow felt 'heard' – more relaxed – and would do what he needed to do to get outside, to feel the air.

A few days later, I received an email from the young man's mother: 'On Monday, when I went to visit Edward, he agreed to some psychological treatment that he'd been adamantly refusing for many months, and because he's done this, the hospital has said he'll be moving to a low secure unit in the next two to three months. As soon as he's there, they'll be looking to move him back into the community. I want to express my heartfelt thanks to Heidi and everyone who was at the workshop on Saturday.'

A sceptic would say it was coincidence, a fluke and great timing. The boy's mother says his decision, made on that Monday, was extremely unlike his previous behaviour. She believes his decision was the direct influence of the group two days prior to that. A course was set in motion by the power of intuition, empathy and mind management.

Frustration

The dictionary defines frustration as 'the feeling of being upset or annoyed as a result of being unable to change or achieve something.' Frustration occurs on the road to mind management as we become stuck between what it is we know and what it is we wish to understand but is a new, unexplored path.

> Intuitive-Sensitives are cautious fellows; they like to have a sense of predictability, rather than take careless risks. This is because something that further stimulates their already overwhelmed nervous system is a lot to process, so they like to know what they're getting into.

This isn't to say their behaviour is cowardly – far from it. Intuitive-Sensitives are incensed by injustice and are the first to risk themselves for a cause they believe in.

Frustration is a normal part of our development, and we see it strongly displayed in a childhood temper tantrum. I have to prevent myself from laughing out loud when I see my youngest son in a moment of frustration, his facial expressions and purity of anger innocently displayed. Frustration teaches us to power on through; it makes us want something and reach for an end result.

However, it's unhelpful when the energy of frustration becomes trapped. Often people see it as a shameful emotion, and many Intuitive-Sensitives in particular have shut it down early in life. Displays of emotion have been programmed as inappropriate, something to be embarrassed by, so when the energy shows as a prelude to intuitive breakthrough, it's bottled up inside, going off like an out-of-date lettuce at the bottom of the fridge.

This kicks up all the goblins and gremlins of the monkey brain (see chapter 5) – and when we're in this state, there isn't much reasoning to be had. We're fearful; we want guaranteed outcomes before we'll take action. The problem is, there are no guaranteed outcomes in life when it comes to aspects of our emotional security.

We have to allow a level of fluidity and develop an ability to let things go… let it be. When we're bound up in the emotion of frustrations that have never had their say, they become toxic feelings that swirl into an emotional paralysis.

When this happens our frustration becomes an internalized experience until it reaches a bursting point. It's at this time, and usually *only* this time for some people, that the frustration is expelled as an inappropriate tirade. As an Intuitive-Sensitive, you'll be frightened by the power of these outbursts, and will therefore keep frustration safely tucked inside.

Over-cooked frustration blocks intuitive progress because it takes us back to the narrowing of focus, of overly left-hemisphere thinking, rather than including the more expansive view of our right-hemisphere. It bubbles inside, making us paranoid. Ever wondered why someone having a rant can never see another person's point of view? This gives you an insight into the answer.

To really understand what mind management is, and its role in our spiritual progress, we have to recognize frustration as an energy that exists to propel intuitive breakthrough, not something that keeps us helplessly paralyzed. It's easier said than done, but one of the simpler routes is to allow yourself to recognize the frustrated child energy: the part that wasn't allowed its full expression.

Iris's story

When I met her Iris was a frightened person. She admitted that her perceptive skills had been present since a young age. She felt she had grown up a gentle and often scared child, who didn't want to trouble anyone. Later in life she was able to admit to herself that living with an often absent father, who spent his days working and his evenings entertaining himself in bars, was emotionally uncomfortable.

Everything Iris experienced in her world had been about pleasing her father, becoming acceptable to him. She began to notice from around the age of eight, that if her father wasn't the centre of attention he'd become moody, angry and on occasion, aggressive. Iris soon learned that it wasn't a good idea to have her own opinions. When her father did something obviously questionable, Iris's mother would seek to silence her daughter, telling her not to make a fuss or draw attention to the contradiction, and making excuses for his behaviour.

Iris had numerous skin complaints that had started very early on, probably due to an intolerance to milk. However, they grew gradually worse as she matured. In her adult years Iris started to question her skin complaints: no medications had worked in the long-term, so she was now searching for her own answers. She began to allow herself the luxury of accessing her inner frustration; she knew it was there but reaching for it felt dangerous somehow. She described it as a desperation for an 'inner scream' but she couldn't possibly vocalize it.

There was a feeling of being able to reach to something inside herself – an invisible hand to help her up, some kind of connection to something kinder, with more meaning – but it remained just beyond her grasp. As Iris tried to reach to this part inside herself, she had a strong sense that it was linked to her father. She'd always known he was difficult, self-centred and demanding, but sometimes there were good days. Blaming him for something, or even considering that he'd had some hand in it beyond the obvious, seemed indulgent, disloyal.

At the end of her tether, Iris decided to allow herself the pain of accessing her frustration – the true reason she felt blocked. From this space flowed images, connections and feelings to early life memory about restriction and her deep disappointment in her father's lack of attention; it was the voice she didn't have.

Iris noticed after this experience that her intuitive instinct seemed to open to new levels. Instead of frightening her, her perception for other people started to propel her. She found a new level of acceptance – an energy beyond frustration.

Iris told me that, within a few months of this exercise, her skin conditions began to clear up. They had been present for decades, but they disappeared without a trace.

Rejection

Guilt and shame are primal, primitive emotions that evolved to ensure our ancestors' survival. They are why the primitive hunter took the food back for his family/tribe to share, rather than eating it all himself, which would have jeopardized their survival. We're heavily programmed to understand guilt and shame, but the issue is we're not meant to keep those feelings long-term. Guilt and shame have become part of the human condition, to keep aspects of ourselves in a low sense of worth; and they are often used by others as a means of control.

One form of guilt and shame is humiliation, and from what I've seen within the groups I've spoken to over the years, this is the Intuitive-Sensitive's number one fear; it's the dreaded emotion we'll do anything to avoid. Recently I heard a story of an Intuitive-Sensitive who set a store buzzer off when she walked past a security tag detector. It happened in two stores of the same name. Afraid that she'd somehow set it off, she refuses to return to the store again.

This might seem like an extreme reaction, but to an Intuitive-Sensitive, the emotional potentials of humiliation are too awful to bear. This person will have been temporarily consumed by the fear she might be accused and punished for something she hadn't done, and the nervous overload is too much to potentially deal with again.

The survival instinct around passivity is strong. Victims of physical assaults often can't fathom why, when they are normally so strong-willed, they flopped into a helpless mess when they were attacked. It's deep within our primitive history, and strongly linked to the animal instinct within us: if we are to question the leader of the 'pride' we must be sure we're strong enough to take over.

If we're not, when it comes to the 'fight' without certainty of absolute backing, we can be sure we'll be humiliated into retreat: the guilt and shame ensuring we leave the tribe altogether, ostracized and never to return.

We see it in other animal groupings – the wounded lion, for example – and this is often why people will ask for backing before confronting something. Another person's support feels vital; we're playing on the primal instincts of territory. If we're not sure we can win, especially when the 'attack' or perceived attack seems to be authoritative, we go into passivity or beat a hasty retreat.

If a child has grown up in a very territorial environment and learned never to question the 'leader of the pack', they'll find it very hard as an adult to let go of a fear of humiliation/rejection. As a child, confronting the pack leader would have been a dangerous move; it would not have been met with a civilized discussion. The child's desires would have been minimized, rejected as unimportant, or worse, they would have been attacked.

When it comes to our own process as adults in the journey towards mind management, the fear of crossing this perceived line in the psyche is incredibly strong. Rejection becomes an enormous red flag, even though, logically, we know the threat isn't there. Therefore, when it comes up as an issue to step over, it's overwhelmingly difficult, even though we know taking the journey across in terms of giving up the fear of rejection leads us towards a deeper sense of peace.

Trust

Trust is a big ask when we have a level of internal stimuli that does anything but trust. Trust is about having a confidence in something or someone. For many Intuitive-Sensitives the initial higher levels of intuition have built up because their trust in the external world has been betrayed. To switch that distrust to trust is a strong adjustment.

At this level, though, trust isn't in anything within the external world; it's an internal adjustment. However, I've seen many Intuitive-Sensitives start their journey looking to the external world, not in people, but a faith in something higher, more powerful than themselves. For some it's given the actual name 'God', or something equal to it; for others it's a new faith or belief in feeling guided by an invisible force, or the belief in angelic assistance. For many, there has been a feeling of a guardian angel of sorts.

As trust develops, this feeling of an external assistance, or guidance, tends to begin to fade, even though it's been comforting and strong. This change doesn't mean it has gone – it means the internal shift has happened, as the feeling has moved from being externalized to being internalized. A deeper reliance and connection with the inner world has therefore meant that the comfort of looking to something of seemingly greater importance is no longer required.

Trust comes as we develop a deeper connection with our own heartfelt values. I recently heard Gregg Braden refer to the scientific discovery that we have 'two brains' – one in our head and the other in the heart. Apparently the 'mind' of the heart acts independently of the brain.

This is a fairly recent discovery, backed by peer-reviewed articles. In terms of trust, the 'heart-mind' triggers a deeper connection to intuitive thought, opening a desire to connect with unconditional love, a form that's difficult to find in another person.

Angels provide a perfect representation, whether real or imagined. This manifestation of unconditional love helps us to find a new or renewed trust, when perhaps little in the external world has offered that.

Engage with unconditional love

In the following exercise, you can use the 'two-brain' method of feeling in the gut area rather than the head.

1. Bring into your mind something that makes you feel uneasy. An example would be worrying about what others think.

2. Feel the emotion in your 'gut'. Clear your thoughts and imagine sending unconditional love to the feeling. Unconditional love means just love, not an expectation of outcome, which would be a 'fix yourself or else' attitude with an expectation of success or failure.

While the 'heart-mind' develops that thought and looks for ways for us to connect with unconditional love, through the experience of trust we begin to make firmer connections with the 'second brain' – the grey matter in our head. The body and head are already connected, not just literally, but through the vagus nerve, which leads from the head to the stomach. Fear messages are known to run between the brain and the stomach, along the two-way street of the vagus nerve.

Studies show that rats became less fearful of open spaces and trying new foods when the gut-to-brain part of the vagus nerve was severed, which suggests the vagus nerve plays more than a minor role when it comes to fear.[1] As we develop a better relationship and understanding of our connection to the 'heart-brain' through unconditional love, in whichever format it chooses to arrive, we build enough trust to deal with the more brutal fears from the gut-to-brain communication. How do we complete the cycle? Through the emergence of and ability to sustain mind management.

Attaining the elusive

In my experience, mind management leads to a quietened inner world and mind peace, but it's an ongoing process rather than an absolute destination. Mind management is the beginning stage of a more meditative journey towards settling your sensitivity and growing your intuitive world into something of huge benefit in your life. Personally, the settling of my sensitivity and opening of my intuitive senses has led me to a very enriched experience of life, while still having both feet firmly planted on the ground.

Mind management is necessary for your intuitive senses to become less random, more organized and 100 per cent more effective. This is the stage where your general thought patterns start to become positive, given the brain's natural tendency to focus on negativity. Our baseline resting state activates a default setting, and one of those functions is to track our environment for possible threats,[2] which keeps us in a state of anxiety and vigilance.

Top that with any early life tensions and your inner world is going to be programmed to react to more and more stimuli. In terms of our primitive history, we had good reason to become anxious, as there was a lot of fear.

Early humans were both predators and prey, and our brain is therefore programmed naturally to detect negative information faster than it processes positive information. We know that as an everyday experience in life, negative headlines sell newspapers, and fearful faces are perceived much more quickly than happy or neutral ones.[3]

> As we know from our own experiences, the hyper-vigilance of being Intuitive and Sensitive means we seem to process negativity even faster, especially given the fact we don't have to even see things physically, we feel them.

Researchers have found that even when they make fearful faces invisible to conscious awareness, the amygdala – the part of the brain responsible for detecting fear and preparing for emergencies – still lights up.[4] And for Intuitive-Sensitives, that lighting up feels like laser lights in a disco.

This is why mind management is crucial – if your intuitive process is to calm down from the disco lights and general sound invasion, it needs to become more organized, progressive and realistic. Not all stimuli are aggressive, yet an undeveloped Intuitive-Sensitive will interpret them as such. This places enormous strain on our physical, emotional and spiritual resources, and both mind and body become saturated to the point of exhaustion.

Training the screaming monkey

The key to mind management is the active training of the monkey mind (see chapter 5). Understanding the stages of resistance, denial, frustration, rejection and finally trust, is the process of gaining a level of communication with the monkey – a means of connection without the monkey attacking you while it feels cornered and frightened.

Our brain, with its animalistic origins, spends its day deciding what to approach and what to avoid. We do this both physically and mentally. For instance, we decide whether to approach a bar of chocolate and push away the guilt, or we pursue self-worth while avoiding shame. Our inner monkey makes decisions based on the past. If it received something nice in the past and encounters the same thing again, it will say it's a 'go towards' experience. If it last had an uncomfortable experience, it will see it as a 'go away from' instruction.

This is what we'll automatically do, without our conscious intervention: we'll go by this default setting unless we're actively participating. The monkey will start screaming if you ask it to proceed forwards when the instruction was previously a 'go away from' and vice-versa. This is probably why we continue to do something when we know it's not good for us. The previous instruction was a 'go towards', perhaps because we associate it with what we expect. It then becomes about resistance when we want to go against it, or our monkey is screaming when we're told to go against it.

A well-trained monkey doesn't scream in your face. But how do you train it? As we know, the incorrect perception is to think you have to get rid of the monkey. That's impossible: it's part of our brain's heritage and it's the primate in all of us.

Our intuitive senses are the overseeing energy, the scout that goes ahead to check the route. They forewarn the monkey of any surprises, dangers and possible attacks, so it doesn't feel startled when it stumbles upon them.

The monkey then learns to expect the unexpected, to predict certain routes on its journey. Intuition helps the monkey to change its perception and begin to trust. It becomes the monkey's friend, not its enemy. Having a well-trained monkey begins with finding it a 'home', a place it feels it can safely retreat to without feeling threatened, where it can relax and feel protected. Intuition has its back.

Creating your monkey's home

I found through years of originally having a very scared, screaming monkey, that intuition came knocking to offer its help. In the initial stages it made its presence very well known. It presented to my monkey very vivid experiences of knowing; it took me through the opening stages of intuition – it couldn't have been more obvious in its approach.

My monkey, running against the bars of its inner cage, was at first terrified of intuition when it arrived. It saw it as something to run away from, to avoid. Intuition though was ethereal, it wasn't solid; it wasn't something you could run at and knock over. It remained consistently present, never leaving my monkey's side, even though my monkey chose to ignore it. Eventually, my monkey began to realize this 'thing' that was present had a consistency about it; it wasn't threatening. Its presence began to make the cage adjust, to feel like a home rather than a prison – a place to come back to that felt nice, safe, and welcoming.

At this point 'monkey' decided to communicate with 'intuition' and stray further from the cage door. It decided to go deep into the jungle, bouncing across territories, its confidence growing because it suddenly felt never alone; it had ethereal 'intuition' up ahead, showing it the routes to take and the experiences to be had. Monkey learned that intuition was its strongest friend in life, its teacher; the part that makes us human.

Summary and action ideas

~ Mind management leads to an inner world of calm communication. The onslaught of Sensitive feelings can be successfully resolved through rebuilding your 'broken vase'.

~ Successful mind management requires us to go through the stages of resistance, denial, frustration, rejection and trust. These lead to a quietened inner world and mind-peace, but it's an ongoing process rather than a destination.

~ For an Intuitive-Sensitive, stimuli is like laser lights in a disco. Hyper-vigilance is our primitive reflex, a hangover from the days when humans were both predators and prey. As a result, the brain is programmed to detect negative information faster than positive. Mind management is the resolution of this.

Chapter 9

Step 3: Make the Transition from Personality to Soul

'Opportunity is missed by most people because it is dressed in overalls and looks like work.'
THOMAS EDISON

Happiness doesn't come from attaining goals – it comes from living a life free of emotional compromise. Goals are simply a marker, a point in the road, they won't give us the feeling of relief we seek. I realized this one rainy day while picking blackberries in the forest with my sons. In that moment I experienced a pure, yet very simple happiness. There was nothing to worry over, nothing to feel invaded by, just the focus of looking for the best black, juicy, ripe berries, free of cobwebs and insects.

Intuitive-Sensitives feel the pain of others' pressures. We conform to what feels comfortable to them, often stepping over the line into self-compromise. We sense their internal pressure, too, the things that make them uncomfortable – from a late night to being upset about something that happened weeks ago.

We take on extra pressure rather than solve the pressure we've already taken on. Often we'll do this by pleasing someone else rather than tending to our own requirements. We do this because we think the right thing to do is to alleviate another person's pressure, but all it does is create more pressure for ourselves.

As our own intuitive process begins to deepen, we need to transform a life of appeasing into a life of serving. And in order to do that, we need to focus on healing the separation between personality and soul.

What's the point of becoming 'conscious'?

Becoming conscious means we're more personally aware of how we impact our world and that of the people around us. We become more aware of what's important to us rather than reacting to what we don't like. Becoming more conscious means becoming happier, more fulfilled and empowered. This is vital when it comes to connecting with the soul and the personality. If we're not self-aware, it's difficult to distinguish between a 'personality panic' and a 'soul push forward'.

Before we look at the definition of 'soul' and 'personality', it's important to realize why you would want to become 'conscious' in the first place – and what 'consciousness' is. There's a generally agreed definition of consciousness: it's the function of knowing, a continuous process of thought and awareness. In my view it's the internal conversation: the level of awareness we have that helps us recognize and admit when we're doing something from fear and when we're engaged in more meaningful actions.

Sometimes though, we confuse the desire to attain something with a path to happiness, only to find the original desire was motivated by fear. When we're 'conscious' we spend less time satisfying the senses and more time feeling content within the framework of what and who we are. That natural framework is a reason for motivation – it doesn't create complacency, it creates a childlike pleasure in the smallest of things.

The trouble is, we're not born that way: it takes time, effort and engagement to train the inner world to attain a higher level of consciousness. The argument comes when we look at consciousness from the viewpoint of cognitive science and its stiff disagreements with spirituality. Neurology holds that everything we think, do, and believe originates purely within the brain. All extra-sensory abilities are either figments of our imagination or a result of neurological processes. This viewpoint means there's no universal intelligence, and everything happens because of biological adjustments and evolution.

Spirituality, on the other hand, sees consciousness as multi-dimensional in origin – it's something that occurs both within and beyond the individual. It's often an experience of gnosis – a deep and certain inner knowing that arises somewhere from the depths of our being.

At some stage in our opening process to the deeply intuitive parts of ourselves, we have a knowing of something yet we're not sure as to its origin. The silent words – which we feel rather than hear – are wise, sometimes prophetic and certainly kind. Within spiritual perspectives the reasons for this may be past soul experiences, including past lives, karmic influence (law of cause and effect) or information 'downloaded' from a more enlightened source.

As they have done for millennia, people need to feel connected to a deeper meaning in life. It's part of our humanity, a route for the empathetic nature to have its expression. A deep desire to feel wholly connected through our emotional world to our environment is, I believe, part of the point of life.

The point therefore in becoming 'conscious' is to enhance your experience of life. I firmly believe people need an idea of faith to feel connected to others, life, and a greater meaning. It isn't enough to have a full awareness of life as an action of the brain, regardless of whether it proves entirely correct that everything can be explained as a neurological function.

Science and mental health

Some Intuitive-Sensitives are concerned that if they reveal they have deeply intuitive or even psychic experiences, they will be marched off to the asylum. They therefore proceed with great caution when starting to open up to their deeper inner world.

Dick Swab, an eminent neurobiologist, says that what are usually explained as spiritual experiences are actually the result of a lack of brain stimulation, to the degree that the brain has started to manufacture events.[1] For example, after a long period of being alone, mountaineers sometimes have vivid experiences of hearing voices, seeing people, or having out-of-body experiences or feeling overwhelmed by deep fear.

Swab goes on to say that the founders of some of the world's major religions had been alone for days in the wilderness, experiencing fear and bright lights, and hearing voices, which is very similar to the mountaineers' experience.

Although I can agree with the neurobiologist's point of view to an extent, I don't believe the explanation is a full one. I've seen many people who don't have a mental illness who suddenly go through the experience of connection to something deeper than themselves.

The intuitive process in the first instance is somewhat subtle and then builds in intensity to startling levels. Intuitive people show no signs of schizophrenia – they do anything but spend long periods alone – yet they have had strong spiritual experiences and insight into others' lives. Neurologists, neurobiologists and neuroscientists, from what I can gather, have little explanation for the ability to see into the life of another person. And Intuitive-Sensitive People are often able to do such things.

This doesn't mean 'cold reading', as the Intuitive-Sensitives capability of directly seeing into a person's life is possible without the person present. There's no opportunity to ask questions or gather any information about the person, so cold reading is impossible. The explanation, in my view, is that energy is present from the outset, hidden in the field of the person who is asking, either consciously or unconsciously. The energy then becomes 'active' for interpretation.

Personally, I see this particularly around people who have been adopted. I'm often asked to intuitively feel the energy of the person's biological family. I'm not claiming to be right every time but certainly on more than one occasion I've recounted information about their biological origin that upon investigation has proven to be correct.

This could be interpreted as being the 'nature' argument – that I'm taking on components of the person in front of me – but on more than one occasion I've not seen, and sometimes not even spoken to, the person who's asking. How then could I possibly know?

The origin of a person is carried in what can be described as their 'energy imprint', regardless of who they've spent time around. The energy imprint consists of their emotional heritage, passed through the generations rather than the person just being a product of their environment.

I find that inherited energy imprint is stronger from the mother's line. This imprint is there clearly for interpretation by those conscious enough to 'see' it. Energy in this format doesn't lie because it isn't tainted by human interaction – it just presents itself as the truth.

Intuitive-Sensitive individuals are radars for this level of truth. In order to see that though, they go through a 'psychic cleansing', inspired by their growing intuitive insight. Unfortunately, this insight is often deeply uncomfortable for the Intuitive-Sensitive, especially in the early stages. They fear being labelled a crackpot or being overly scrutinized for something they didn't choose as a capability, it just happened upon them.

An intuitive voice or psychosis?

Neurobiologists believe that 'hearing voices' signifies the onset of psychosis rather than an engagement with a stronger level of consciousness. And in many instances it is. Over the years I've come across cases of some people who, upon entering a time of deep stress, began to hear what they believed to be the voices of the dead.

Their experiences are indeed more in keeping with a psychotic episode. In what I've seen, their view of 'hearing a voice' is accompanied by agitation, and at times the voice is either overly holy, or it tells them they are bad or evil.

Functional brain scans show that even those who 'hear voices', yet are not psychotic, have a brain that lights up in a similar area to those who have psychosis. The Broca's area, responsible for language production, the primary auditory cortex and the Wernicke's area (responsible for hearing, processing and comprehending language) are, not surprisingly, impacted. The energy for interpretation would have to be processed somewhere and yes, it would have to be processed through the brain, but it doesn't necessarily originate there.

If it were simply the case, as many neurobiologists believe, that consciousness begins and ends in the brain, it doesn't explain how many Intuitive-Sensitives are able to perceive the lives of people they've never met as though simply receiving feedback from their own brain. Swab says that, unlike psychotic patients, healthy people who 'hear voices' can control the voices they hear. I would disagree.

> There are many Highly Intuitive people who have a strong instinct for something, who 'hear a voice' that has proven to help them or someone else out of a situation. It's happened to me on countless occasions; I'm not psychotic (I've checked) and I don't have a family history of schizophrenia, yet the interpretations and how I get to them, continue to surprise me enormously.

On one occasion I met a woman who asked me to help her unravel a life situation she had that seemed to be repeating itself. I can't remember the exact details, as it was some while afterwards that she came up to me at an event to confirm what had happened. I'd said to her that I kept seeing a famous painting in my mind – it was one I couldn't remember the name of but I knew it as 'The lady of the lake'.

I told the woman that the painting was somehow connected to the family pattern she was currently trying to solve around property and money. The next time I saw her, she told me she'd had no idea at the time what I was talking about. 'The lady of the lake' had no meaning for her; she'd never heard of or seen the painting and couldn't recall any family situations around a painting.

However, she couldn't wait to tell me that, some weeks after talking to me, she'd gone to see her father to take him for a day out. In the car he suddenly started talking about an old neighbour and an argument over property – I believe it was something to do with a sitting tenant. Through him recalling this relationship he mentioned that this woman was known as 'The lady of the lake'. His daughter was very quick to point out, when recalling the story, that she had not seen or spoken to her father between my interaction with her and her visit to him.

I can't see how this example could be my 'hearing my own brain'. Many Intuitive-Sensitives have had such scenarios that cannot be rationally explained. It's an incredible pressure to have the lives of others impacting your own inner world in a very vivid manner, especially if you don't understand what's happening.

But what is it that happens for these people? It is, I believe, the process of becoming conscious, the ability to see a truth, a neutralized, untarnished view – a desire man has hunted for centuries.

Intuitive-Sensitivity and Kabbalah

As I said earlier, I've never met an Intuitive-Sensitive who asked for their experience to happen to them. I don't believe that any of us start out on a soul-seeking path; it happens upon them as part of their experience. They need answers to certain questions – they realize their world is changing and there's little they can do about it.

Whatever they chase in the external world gives no relief; their world eventually turns inwards to find that peace comes from knowing their deepest nature, harnessing the power of who they are. This isn't done as a glossy show or through party tricks – the majority just want to get on with their lives and connect to the deeper truth they feel is part of their life experience. Call this a crisis of the nervous system if you wish, or consider perhaps that there are other explanations.

As a person becomes more self-aware they become a more conscious individual. As this happens, the 'personality' and 'soul' start to unite – the person then often feels that the structure in the familiar aspects of their life begins to break down. It starts to transform into something new. The old life at a very personal level is impacted and changes drastically. The experience is so personal, that for many it's incredibly difficult to articulate.

To help explain this journey of change in the inner world, I've found that the 'Tree of Life' is an extremely helpful tool. The Tree of Life helps to show what can feel like huge personal change. For some people, the changes can feel unrecognizable when compared to aspects of their earlier life. This can be disconcerting, but the Tree of Life helps to make it clear and meaningful. We get to better understand the learning examples, the opportunities to strengthen the core spirit of who we are.

The Tree of Life has its roots in the ancient beliefs of Kabbalah, a Hebrew tradition based on the 22 letters of the Hebrew alphabet. I don't profess to know the complete ins and outs of the Hebrew tradition; I believe that's inappropriate as I've no Jewish roots. Rather, I see it as a way of helping to explain what consciousness and the process of it is, regarding the connection between soul and personality and what that feels like.

Within Kabbalist traditions, the law of the universe exists always as a polarity, a kind of push and a pull at all times. In this context you cannot have creativity without destruction – the two operate at the same time, in the same space. In other words, you cannot reach a feeling of blissful enlightenment while living your life avoiding pain.

Kabbalah has a way of communicating what consciousness means – beauty as to the laws of nature and spirituality in a space away from the purely biological or heavily religious interpretations of good and evil, the pure and the damned. Essentially, the meaning of Kabbalah is the combining of personality (man) with the soul (God); the beliefs are tied into what we do here in our physical world and how that impacts 'God', rather than God being a powerful, all-knowing being who wields a big stick.

The basis of Kabbalist mystical teaching is *The Zohar* – a commentary on the Hebrew Torah (the five books of Moses) that's designed to give people with spiritual perception all the spiritual states they'll experience as their soul evolves. To those without spiritual knowledge, *The Zohar* reads as a collection of allegories.

The literal interpretation of *The Zohar* is 'In the beginning it created God', meaning infinity. A universal intelligence is the true reality of God. This perception fits with much of what many Intuitive-Sensitives believe to be their reality – i.e. a connection to an infinite wisdom, feeling part of it yet separated, with a longing for the peace of the combination of the two.

As we pursue the balance of the individual personality and soul combination, this is what we strive for. It's within our framework to do good and to contribute – a strange realization dawns that our actions somehow impact the flow down of balance, the connection to an infinite intelligence.

The 'Tree of Life' is seen as a version of God's body – the Infinite's energy system, for want of a better way of putting it. Even a basic understanding of it gives rise to insight into our own motivations to live a more emotionally rewarding life. It's the opening to 'contact' with our deeper mind.

I use the Tree of Life not as the Kabbalah interpretation but as a way of identifying life's lessons – establishing the distinction between personality and soul, followed by the combining of them. This gives an immediate insight into how we work through something in life. This formation 'talks' to the Intuitive-Sensitive in a way they understand.

Managing the transition from personality to soul

In my description of 'the personality' – a way to describe the process of awakening for the Intuitive-Sensitive Person – I use aspects of Kabbalah (above), Eastern philosophy, and components of Eastern traditions, all mixed with a splash of Transpersonal Psychology. The latter integrates spiritual experiences with modern psychology – Transpersonal Psychology is really psychology for the soul seeker. I've found that this blend talks to the Intuitive-Sensitive and enhances their understanding of their place in the world.

The personality is the 'I' of who we are. It's the selfish part of the self, concerned with its survival and self-preservation. The selfish aspect is required in order to survive the challenges of the physical world; it defines us from others and it gives us our identity. This part of our inner world is constructed from our physical and emotional history, both during our lifetime and inherited from our parental line. The personality feels the emotional world; it's the 'point' of us being physical. Its separation and identity gives reason for us to be alive in this world.

An unmanaged personality believes itself to be the main object of importance. It's competitive and jealous; it strives to be noticed in a world of personalities, desperate to be seen. We could also refer to it as the ego.

This description makes the personality sound like a self-serving nightmare that has its own idea of preservation as its priority. From the view of the physical world, separated from the awareness of the rest of ourselves (the deeper parts of the Tree of Life), we are the only thing in the world of importance. The human mind, the most intelligent of the animal kingdom, is the king of the castle.

This is where we live in a world of protecting only what serves us; it's the reason why we start and don't finish things, why we only have a half-hearted view of protecting something for longevity, because once we're gone we don't believe it affects us. The personality, though, will want to protect the interests of its children, simply because it adheres to a biological force in operation rather than a spiritual one. A spiritual force would view everyone as an extension of itself: therefore we would see every person as our son, daughter, brother, sister, etc. We would feel a strong need to treat all equally.

The personality, however, doesn't see people as the collective: it sees through the lens of personal gain and protection, which means it has a biological urge to protect its children and in the long term, protect itself. This doesn't mean it's wrong for doing that – it just means it's the way we're shaped in order to honour our survival in the physical world. In terms of the less positive traits, the personality is the source of procrastination, co-dependence, infatuation, fear and glee.

For the Intuitive-Sensitive Person, the personality has often not had the opportunity to become self-serving to the extent that it should have done. Many Intuitive-Sensitives have at some stage in their life had to 'serve' someone with an out-of-control personality: one that's only seen itself in a world where it hasn't had the concept of another. The Intuitive-Sensitive has therefore activated their self-preservation in a different way.

To become more aware of 'personalities' they have decided they must be of service to the more dominant force – to people-please, to see themselves in many cases as unworthy. The strong characteristics of the more dominant personality in another have then become abusive. In many instances they are consciously abusive. They have taken advantage of the Intuitive-Sensitive's self-protection mechanism to serve the out-of-control personality.

As a method of self-protection the Intuitive-Sensitive has stepped on eggshells, done whatever they think the other person has wanted, in order at some point to be accepted. The conflict comes as the soul begins to awaken. It begins to trigger into existence the Intuitive's consciousness, the connection with the rest of themselves.

Specks of intuitive insight begin to filter through. This insight is subtle, it's a knowing without knowing that grows over a period of time. It's at this point the intuitive mind begins to question what it can start to see as unkind or unfair. It's the start of a flourishing into deep integrity. The issue is that the deep integrity is always towards others first, when in fact the true progress begins when the integrity is directed towards the self.

As we learned earlier, it isn't always the case that an Intuitive-Sensitive has been on the receiving end of some form of psychologically or emotionally abusive behaviour in order for the intuition spark to grow. But it is the case that they are born with the Sensitive capacity, which has to be present for the intuitive senses to flourish.

These are not fleeting experiences of psychic insight, they are more permanent – a natural instinct for other people, a caring nature and an ability to help others heal. As the personality becomes increasingly aware of the soul stirring, the person then develops a strong desire to transform what isn't working; they feel they need to adjust their life to one of contribution, of higher learning and selflessly 'giving back' in one way or another.

This process may have been triggered by the Intuitive-Sensitive's own desire to heal themselves. In fact, in many instances this is the case. The drive for 'personality' and 'soul' to meet is driven by a desire for unity within the self, the intuitive connection having in some instances been ignited by a wish to finally feel loved. Intuition at a deeper level, beyond the everyday, is the experience of unconditional love, a settled and peaceful inner world eased from the pressure of anxiety.

When the issues are faced, the relationship between personality and soul deepens in connection. The inner world becomes quieter inside. You come to realize that although you've always been inside there, you've been overwhelmed by a barrage of thoughts, emotions and sensations that have drawn upon your consciousness.

It's at this point that the personality is prepared to melt into the role it was meant to have: to provide its service as the protector of the physical body and to work with the discovery of the quieter, non-stressed component we refer to as the soul.

Flourishing into soul

Flourishing into soul means going deep into the layers created by the personality, as a means to hide from pain. Within the journey of the 'consciousness line' through the Tree of Life, there are three crossing points of the paths created. These signify the 'dark night of the soul' part to life: the journey to ourselves that no-one seeking a deeper meaning can avoid.

At the core of this pattern we dance around life to avoid the discomfort – we try to stay busy with our friends, our work; we hide in their acceptance. Every layer is attached to the original pain; flourishing within the soul energy is the acknowledgement that pain is there. None of us is immune to it. The journey of the personality is to transcend it, but in order to know of its existence the soul reveals it.

> The soul is the spark or essence of who you are – your expression in the world that isn't constricted by worrying about what others perceive or think. Those who refuse to handle emotional pain react by closing their mind. They build a complete psychological structure around their closed energy, making sure as best they can that no-one can penetrate it.

This is painful to the Intuitive-Sensitive – the sensation of feeling other people's hidden and protected world is strong for them. People rationalize why they're right, why the other person is wrong and why they should be listened to. A wall of denial keeps them enslaved to their fear.

When the soul connection is deepening for the Intuitive-Sensitive, the fear path becomes stronger. Fearful experiences are positioned in front of you, and life may suddenly present its extremities. These are there not as a test, but as a way for your inner world to finally transcend the fear of fear. It's as though all of your history arrives in person at your door.

The soul and your history on the doorstep

As the relationship between 'soul' and 'personality' begins to deepen, whatever is psychologically in the way has the habit of presenting itself for processing. Subconscious patterns left behind a long time ago reappear, often in a more exaggerated form. The nightmarish boss you had 10 years ago reappears in your new boss, only significantly worse. The emotionally immature ex-partner shows up in a new one. The list is seemingly endless and personal.

What's actually happening is a cleansing of the emotions, a tidying up of your self-esteem, but it feels as though the fear is once again in full flow. The soul 'descending' into the everyday world requires a tidy up. The tidying is like purchasing a new sofa for your sitting room. When you buy a new sofa do you stack it on top of the old, tatty one? When guests come into your house do they need a step ladder to climb on top of your stack of sofas?

It doesn't make sense to buy a new sofa and stack it on the old one yet metaphorically people try to do that in their inner world. Hence the reason the soul's awakening has standards. It doesn't want to stack the sofa – it wants it to leave the building, because its presence no longer suits the environment. Trying to move it to another room means the old, tatty presence is still in your house – you just moved it to the side.

When your inner world has too many old sofas, the soul's energy is too strong to be denied: it wants the sofas out. It then has the habit of throwing all the old sofas out into the street. A growing intuition has been present for long enough to know that you need to get rid of the sofas, but haven't got around to it, or were too scared to release the old favourites. It's only when the 'soul' has had enough of the 'personality's hoarding that it gets forceful enough to change the circumstances.

This is the point when the Intuitive-Sensitive feels an internal change is inevitable, a realization that the external world isn't going to make them happy, and that happiness grows from the inside-out. Self-esteem doesn't happen upon you – you have to work at developing it. The realization dawns that others won't respect you unless you work to gain a level of self-respect.

Emotional unity

At this stage of the Intuitive-Sensitive's development the personality and soul begin the process of no longer feeling as though they are separate entities. A feeling of emotional unity starts to happen. Some of this comes in a spontaneous way – the inner world triggering elements of external change – but the majority of the adjustment is conscious.

But how is the change conscious when 'soul' is seemingly part of the unconscious? I've seen, through my own experience and that of others I've helped along the journey, that faith is the great connector. As the personality of who we are begins to develop a faith in the soul's existence, what has previously been a conflicting energy, one frightened of the other, begins to unite in an effort to move forward.

The active development of intuition provides that faith: a process seemingly initially triggered by a brain mechanism or consciousness outside the self to protect the individual from the impact of emotional trauma. The development of it leads to what, for me, has been a permanent state of peace, even in a storm. How do you get there? I'm a firm believer you should honour your fear, not aim to destroy it.

Connecting soul and personality

The following exercise will help you gently to experience the essence of any currently unconscious fears by temporarily 'feeling them'. When an unconscious fear becomes conscious (through you feeling it) the feeling has no choice but to lose energy and dissolve. In life, we generally try to avoid fear.

We mistakenly believe that doing this means it doesn't exist, but the truth is when we feel it properly, for the few minutes it actually takes, fear comes into perspective and resolves itself. The steps below will help take you through this process:

1. Think of what's bothering you the most right now in your life.

2. Let the feeling of it rise in your body, and remain focused on what it is.

3. Let the fear *grow* in your body (usually at this point we distract ourselves).

4. Feel in your body (not in your thoughts) where the emotion sits.

5. Focus on the feeling, switching everything else off. Your breathing will become faster and anxiety will rise, but keep with the feeling.

6. As the feelings of terror rise (if you get deep enough into the feeling it will be a terror of abandonment), have faith in and kindness for yourself to stick with it.

7. The feelings will subside to the point of distraction – you'll start to think of something else. Repeat the process until the original issue no longer has 'energy'.

Summary and action ideas

∾ Personality is the everyday self, and the soul is the spark or essence of who we are. Old patterns resurface as the soul and personality begin to deepen their relationship. This leads to a cleansing of the emotions. Drama in the Intuitive-Sensitive's life releases emotions and the inner world becomes quiet.

∾ The journey of the personality is to transcend pain but to know of its existence: the soul reveals it. Going into the soul means actively moving through life's pain.

∾ To understand the soul, you must be prepared to feel the things that have upset you. To acknowledge them means to release them.

Chapter 10

Step 4: Cope with Others and Their Power Struggles

'As we go through life, we carry not only our own fear but that of our ancestors.'

Much of what we learn about the world has been passed down through the generations: the belief systems of what's right and wrong; what should make us happy or sad; which jobs to take; the careers to forge. Whether this happens through cross-generational social imprinting or what's known as 'epigenetic inheritance' (the passing forward of our ancestors' experiences rather than traditional genetics) remains a largely open question.

My own experience is that there's some kind of energetic memory storage that impacts how we as Intuitive-Sensitives deal with other people and their power struggles, which are how people assert their authority. Not all of how we process these feelings through the nervous system so vividly comes from our own immediate history.

Materialists (theorists who believe that physical matter is the only reality) believe, for example, that all religious or spiritual decisions come from our background: an indoctrination rather than something dictated by choice or experience. Apparently, our receptivity to spirituality is 50 per cent genetically determined, and our parental religion is imprinted on our brain circuitries in much the same way as language.[1]

If this is the case then I should be an atheist with the view that all spirituality is mumbo jumbo. In fact, I've more of a multi-faith fascination and a deeper interest in spiritual experiences than either of my parents would ever have considered.

If it's the case that information is passed on through the generations without conscious knowledge, then it's possible that my spiritual interests have come from some of my more distant relatives – people I never met and with whom my parents had little or no contact.

My grandmother once mentioned to me in adulthood, long after my own interests had developed, that my great, great aunts had had a very strong penchant for spiritual experiences, theosophical philosophy and intuitive insight. She mentioned how they were interested in all kinds of things, from Buddhism to Hindu culture.

> If it's true that our genes are altered through ancestral habits, lifestyles, and health, this would explain why Intuitive-Sensitives find themselves having a tidy-up of a past they were not conscious they had.

Scientific research into the Dutch *Hongerwinter* (hunger winter) of 1944, a famine that took place in the German-occupied part of the Netherlands towards the end of World War II, showed interesting results. It was found that not only were the infants who survived the famine more susceptible to health problems, but these children's own offspring, even though well-fed in pregnancy, were born significantly underweight. The famine had seemingly impacted and 'emotionally' scarred the DNA.

Since the early 1950s DNA has been thought of as nature's blueprint, the detailed chromosomes passed genetically from one generation to the next. It hasn't been largely considered that there's an emotional passing of information from one generation to another: a warning or danger signal passed through the generations and lived out in those further down the line. To put it bluntly, your great-grandparents made lifestyle choices that impact your emotional and physical health today.

The real reason we're afraid of authority

But how does this relate to Intuitive-Sensitives? I believe we experience a patch in our development in which it feels as if we're having to go through some kind of release of our ancestors' past psychological history. It's a process beyond logical sense yet it's very real to our developmental experience.

It's as though the foundational structure, the 'DNA' almost, is going through a cleansing. It's at this time that we experience an increase in the power struggles of other people. Such instances create an enormous strain on the Sensitive nature.

I believe there are more Intuitive-Sensitive individuals wandering around the planet than is realized. Two world wars in recent generations will have created an influx of first-, second- and third-generational babies born with a right-brain preference. A need for hyper-vigilance, through mothers having to negotiate the pressures of war and their off-spring born into stress, will have brought into the world children who are pre-programmed for a more delicate nervous system.

As the Intuitive-Sensitive flows within the framework that works for their more vigilant brain – one that seeks to take in the wider picture (right-hemisphere) than a narrow focus (left-hemisphere) – they feel in charge of their own healing. As this happens, so does the release of the old coding stored from previous generations. This change brings to the fore the Intuitive-Sensitive's hidden cross-generational fear of authority, or a perceived authority, regardless of whether or not they were brought up in a bully environment.

The largest generation currently inhabiting the planet (Baby Boomers) carry the authority residue associated with wars that impacted the world. In order for our self-authority to surface it's as though we're meant to be releasing this stored history within the deepest parts of our physical life and cells.

And for this to happen, we have to have it consciously presented, hence the reason that at some point or another the Intuitive-Sensitive finds themselves having to resolve a very significant dispute. Not of a trivial nature over neighbourhood boundaries, say, but a re-arrangement of their own.

Carrier consciousness

Carrier consciousness is a term used within Indian mysticism and theosophical philosophy to describe a formation of the energy body that carries the consciousness of an individual from life to life. The energy body of carrier consciousness becomes larger and more defined as the human psyche advances through its 'soul lessons' – meaning what we feel in this world we're here to learn.

Soul lessons are not always pleasant lessons; often we learn deeply from what has challenged us the most. Carrier consciousness is spoken of as the 'auric egg' – the living light of the spiritual body.

This energy, or carrier, body, although thought of as invisible to the naked eye, exists as a glowing body of light around each person. In esoteric terms, it's described as the light body. The belief is that, as our consciousness grows, so does the light body. The carrier body is said to contain the energy of the soul's consciousness. Through our lifetime, information is stored in this energetic imprint to be passed on as a learning experience – not only to our next 'incarnation' but also along our genetic lineage. It's the building of soul experience in a human body.

The carrier body therefore retains the previous information and experience to feed the current life with the information of the past. This information remains largely unconscious until we have sufficient awareness – or consciousness – in the present time to recall aspects of the stored life memory. The clearing of the past brightens the carrier body, thus increasing the size of the auric egg.

Release areas are what we need to let go of. The release areas show as several areas of life, one of them being the release of early life emotional experiences that have stored hurt in the 'personality'. Psychologically, we would refer to that as suppressed memories impacting current decisions we're making.

This would show in many different areas, such as questions over the type of relationship we're in, if it's healthy or unhealthy for us to continue putting energy into it, as well as other areas such as figuring out how we solve a personal addiction – whether it's to a substance or a person. Addictions show in many formats – they are things we can't control. They might be a relationship we can't let go of, food, shopping and of course the obvious ones.

Other areas would be possible past-life memories that hold up the present.

The belief is that, as we become more conscious of our soul's movement and lessons moving forwards, the carrier body increases not only in size but becomes more defined. For Intuitive-Sensitives this feels as though old memories we have no recollection of come to the surface. Some may say it's purely a trauma exercise: a post-traumatic stress beginning to release itself in symbolic formats.

Whether carrier consciousness is real or imagined, I've found it to be a very effective way of feeling, and therefore addressing, components of the boundary issues every Intuitive-Sensitive finds themselves going through at some stage on their path.

Boundary issues tend to be where we draw a line in the sand between where we end and another person begins. If we have poor boundaries, we usually find our kindness being taken advantage of.

The awareness of this spiritual route alone helps an Intuitive-Sensitive to realize some of the threats to their progress that they'll routinely find themselves up against. It helps us to recognize the need for better boundaries, rather than skipping that part and worrying too much about what others think – overly people-pleasing.

In their 'natural' habitat, the Intuitive-Sensitive finds their own company a preferable state of affairs, yet they still, when the carrier consciousness energy is very present, find themselves in the presence of another's power play. Why does this happen? Other people's power plays can significantly impact us because there is something unhealed in the carrier consciousness.

Jiva – the healing tool

When we come across another's power play it's all well and good for people to say, 'Set your boundaries'. It seems obvious that if someone asks too much of us we should say 'no' or moderate the request to what we can manage. To a Sensitive individual, setting boundaries is like travelling to the moon on the bus: how do we logically do it? When our sensory world is consistently being invaded by stimuli we didn't ask to be around, short of living life as a recluse, it's difficult for us to set boundaries and remain among life while working on our inner world.

One thing I find it useful for the Intuitive-Sensitive to link with in order for the boundary issue to become more realistic is Jiva – a Sanskrit term for the immortal essence of a living thing. With Jiva, the carrier body accelerates its progress. This means, as the Intuitive-Sensitive accesses more of the essence of who they are, building their intuitive links, the Jiva becomes stronger and the carrier body moves its lessons faster.

From an energetic standpoint this is why many Intuitive-Sensitives find their inner emotional world suddenly accelerating through the 'lessons' of exaggerated power plays. People exaggerate their power plays by forcing their ideals onto how others should 'be' in order to satisfy their own requirements, rather than accepting how they are.

> Jiva is what produces the vital energy of a person: their vibrancy, their mojo. When this has been suppressed through earlier life experiences it begins to build as the intuitive senses are actively used.

When the Jiva energy body is healthy, it produces more Jiva than necessary, a radiating vitality. This helps to supply the deficiencies of others who don't have enough. Unconsciously, it's the Jiva vitality that Sensitives give to others that is the reason why they'll constantly feel so exhausted around some people. Those who haven't enough Jiva absorb it like a sponge from those who have. And Sensitives find themselves giving away a lot of Jiva.

When the Jiva vitality is strong, even if you're a Sensitive, it means less tiredness in the company of others. When you combine the will and imagination aspects of the inner world, it equals strong Jiva energy. The combination helps to create an enhanced protection method from the draining involved from other people.

Building Jiva increases your emotional strength and healing capacity, and this impacts how you process the moods of other people, the effects of stress, and your involvement with emotional dynamics you don't wish to be part of but have found yourself to be around.

We build Jiva through releasing what drains us of energy (negativity) while feeling strong enough to no longer take on someone else's energy. The stronger the Jiva in terms of vitality, the easier it is to no longer take on the responsibilities of another as though they were our own. Empathy then operates at a different level – it's no longer based on releasing someone else's anguish, instead it becomes about noticing someone else's anguish enough for them to feel safe enough to release it for themselves. This is the core of what I call 'observing without absorbing'.

Healthy Jiva propels the carrier body through setbacks and stagnation. This then builds the auric egg, the light body. For the Sensitive individual it gives a deeper understanding of what consciousness means and a stronger sense of the true self. This way of understanding things helps lead the person to a more highly developed sense of self-esteem and the confidence to follow their own path.

They have a way of developing their understanding of their sensitivity without having to link it to a person as such. This takes the pressure off feeling they have to adjust to be approved of. If building confidence, self-esteem and reducing the level of uncomfortable sensitivity can be achieved through 'energy' rather than negotiating people and logical reasoning, it's generally their preference, especially if they've come from a foundational background of unreasonable behaviour that has impacted their capacity to deal with power plays.

Jiva helps us deal with power plays because it's the energy change that alters things, rather than having to confront a power-player. If we confront someone who feels their identity relies on their ability to wield power, they will strike a harder emotional blow in order to remain in charge.

This is often too much for the Intuitive-Sensitive, because they don't want to have to filter something that feels aggressive, even if on the outside it appears 'friendly'. When we have enough Jiva, the power-player feels less inclined to even try for a power play. Why? The Intuitive-Sensitive doesn't 'feel' vulnerable enough to manipulate.

Humiliation and the narcissistic household

As I mentioned earlier, I've noticed that many Intuitive-Sensitives, especially the naturally very intuitive ones, have a history of walking on eggshells in their early life environments. They have certainly developed an overly refined capability of understanding others, usually to their own detriment. These people often have some of the health issues associated with Sensitive people, but in exaggerated forms.

They are the extremely exhausted; the ones with rare health complaints and symptoms that health professionals cannot identify. They have tumours in odd and unexpected places: I've seen adrenal tumours, thyroid tumours and numerous instances of Lupus-related illness, all of which are not your everyday health complaints. But why is there such a high instance of such unusual illness in these types of Sensitives?

I believe it's due to an internal terror that has hounded them their entire life. This terror cannot be specifically identified – the wolf has no identity, no face – yet they do know they want to avoid power and power issues at all costs. If asked they will, usually under pressure, admit to having had a parental figure who was 'harsh at times, but knew what was good for me', or one who was 'critical, but I've learned to live with that'.

Research shows that the adult children of narcissists have a hard time admitting it was an unacceptable environment. Why? Denial is the name of the game in a narcissist household. The children of such environments learn to live with the rules but never stop being confused or pained by them.

We are all narcissistic to some extent – it means that our main concern is self-preservation. When narcissism is pathological, though, the narcissist has a much more extreme sense of self-importance. They will lack empathy and sympathy, and they'll generally demand their needs are met over and above all other people. This will show as dramatic behaviour, mocking others or heavy criticism with the intention of making sure a person doesn't get to be 'bigger' than they are.

They will also criticize someone in an attempt to make sure they're so weak they won't leave them. Often, a narcissist's greatest fear is living alone. Narcissism is more common than we think: many Intuitive-Sensitives have honed their intuitive skills in a narcissistic household in which they had to become very attuned to the narcissist's moods and their need for attention.

There's a block to an emotional access around their parents: the child feels invisible in a visible world; they feel unheard, unseen and devoid of feeling nurtured. They feel bound to the family secret of 'don't tell the outside world, pretend all is fine here.' They are tied in the image of a family of perfection – no problems, always putting on the smile.

Effective communication was a no-no in their family. Communication was never direct – they discovered they were the source of someone's annoyance via someone else in the family. Sibling rivalry was encouraged, and communication only came in the form of anger or rage. 'The typical adult from a narcissistic family is filled with unacknowledged anger, feels like a hollow person, feels inadequate and defective, suffers from periodic anxiety and depression, and has no clue about how he or she got that way.'[2]

Not all Intuitive-Sensitives come from a narcissistic household, but if you experience any of the following feelings, it's likely that you did:

- ∽ You have a chronic need to please.

- ∽ Most of the time, you can't identify your own feelings, wants or needs.

- ∽ You need constant validation, or feel that bad things are your lot and that good things only occur through luck or a mistake.

~ You tremble at the thought of being humiliated.

~ You won't complain when something is unacceptable, in case you're seen as a whiner or complainer.

If this is your reality, healing it becomes a very scary concept. For addressing and admitting the family pain – the secret – even to yourself, means a disloyalty punished by humiliation.

Harriet's story

Harriet remembers vividly how, when she was a child, her father would occasionally be very nice. He'd say nice things about her to other people, but never to her face. A quiet child, Harriet tried to be as unassuming as possible.

One day though she riled the tiger in her father. He'd returned home from work and it was clear that someone had annoyed him. It was time to take it out on Harriet. He wouldn't often leave physical marks, but the emotional marks were always significant. He began to poke at Harriet, trying to aggravate her into a 'play-fight' – something he liked to do. It normally involved light punches followed by one that was too hard.

She'd complain, and he'd say she needed to toughen up, be taught how to see the real world. Harriet would then appease her father and play-fight a little harder until it gave him the excuse to pin her down and 'play-slap' her face.

On one such occasion Harriet had had enough. She forced her hands free and scratched her father's face, digging her nails deep, her chest heaving with frustration and suppressed pain. Her father didn't see this as a sign he was going too far, though, he saw red – no-one, and certainly not Harriet, was to scratch his face. Harriet was furious – she had found it within herself to fight back this once. At 12 years old she felt she should now be able to define her own boundaries.

Harriet's father, displeased with his daughter's response and shocked to see her standing up for herself, still felt he was entitled to release his aggression on her, because someone had dared to challenge him at work. He saw fit to humiliate his daughter as her punishment and his release. Late in the evening, on a freezing February night, he threw Harriet out in the garden and locked the door. On her way out, she was called all manner of things – from ungrateful, to a nasty little girl.

Harriet didn't dare bang on the door; she didn't dare scream her frustration. Instead she retreated to the bottom of the garden, where she belonged, in shock and suffering a deep emotional pain and numbness. Around an hour later, her mother came to find her. She was sat huddled with the dog, which had also been thrown out for trying to defend her. Harriet knew what her mother would say: 'Go and apologize to your father – you shouldn't have done that.'

Not all narcissistic households are steeped in physical violence like Harriet's, but nonetheless, the threat of it makes it tough for these types of Intuitive-Sensitive to handle power, even their own. There's a tremendous fear of the consequences around releasing the people-pleaser in them – the person who takes care of every other need but their own.

This is why, I believe, especially in these types of Intuitive-Sensitive, the strong connection to the intuitive senses begins to develop. This is something that they can feel safe with: an unconditional connection, a love they don't have to rely on from another. This is why using the framework of carrier consciousness and the Jiva energy works for them. They feel free, often for the first time in their life, to truly make their own choices.

How to step into your own power, not a power play

Understanding power plays and healing your own vulnerability around them as an Intuitive-Sensitive comes from owning your own feelings of let-down, humiliation and family history: whether it's first- or second-generational dysfunction.

The sidelining of uncomfortable feelings is dangerous, not only to your growth, but to your emotional wellbeing. Maintaining the uncomfortable energy as a connection to shame keeps you worrying about everyone else, disconnected from your own authenticity.

For the Intuitive-Sensitive, the opening of the soulful connection in the inner world, through the symbolism and energetic responses that seem to want to connect more spontaneously through the accessibility of carrier consciousness and the Jivic energy field, gives a point of authentic connection that's part of the physical world but isn't reliant on it.

Stepping out of the everyday world, separating ourselves from reality, isn't an option. It leads clearly to mental health issues. Pain, humiliation and dissociated feelings are cut off to the extent they have no option but to express negatively.

Your truly intuitive self can only see truth. Intuition isn't a world of superstition, mixing potions or vexing people, it's an expression of truth. As Sensitive individuals, a normal part of our everyday world is being prepared to face our own truth.

At times, facing this may mean admitting and resolving in our inner world the power plays we've perhaps experienced throughout our lives, but have mistaken as love. We can't make our sensitivity go away; believe me, throughout various periods in my life, I've tried! We can, though, allow ourselves to flourish within its beauty, to understand its vulnerabilities and negotiate rather than kick head-on, or avoid, the power plays presented before us.

The protection from power plays comes from working on the inner world – not trying to fend off the outer world, licking the wounds and hiding in shame. It's about building connections with part of your inner world you've not seen before, but is independent of a reliance on other people's opinions.

Actively connecting with this part of ourselves means accepting and at times transcending, an emotional truth linked to our past. So rather than focus on trying to be 'enough', which leaves us wide open to others and their power plays, we must realize ourselves that we are already enough.

Resolving power plays

1. Close your eyes and focus on your breathing.

2. Allow your inner world to become more present as your mind settles and becomes quieter.

3. Think of someone whose behaviour, past or present, feels as though it's an assertion of power over you.

4. Feel the solar plexus (the stomach area) clench with emotional tension. As it clenches, your breathing will become shallower. You may even be holding your breath. Let yourself breathe slowly.

5. Imagine that clenched feeling is your hand around a soft ball. In your mind, let your hand around the ball release, and let the ball bounce back to shape.

Summary and action ideas

∾ Emotional information passes from one generation to another through behavioural epigenetics. This impacts the Intuitive-Sensitive's way of handling other people and their power struggles.

∾ Carrier consciousness is a term used in Indian mysticism to describe the carrying of a person's consciousness from life to life. Other people's power plays can impact us because of something unhealed in the carrier consciousness.

∾ We can use the tool of Jiva to create emotional boundaries. Jiva is Sanskrit for the immortal essence of a living thing. Building Jiva can help our vitality, mojo and emotional strength.

∾ Protection from power plays comes from working on the inner world.

Chapter 11

Step 5: Access Your Super-Intuitive State

'The only real valuable thing is intuition.'
ALBERT EINSTEIN

As Intuitive-Sensitives, our intuition provides a view of life we cannot rationally justify, yet it opens doors and creates happiness. The flow of the intuitive mind is peaceful; it's very present in our physical world, and it certainly isn't something we have to go and get. We do, though, need to step out of what's in the way – and that's usually ourselves.

When we're in our intuitive expression we find a knowing without thinking – a place where anxiety is lost and replaced by a quietness of thought, a gentleness that nothing on the outside can touch. The great Swiss psychiatrist and psychologist Carl Jung referred to intuition as 'perception via the unconscious': a use of a sense that brings forth ideas, images often presented as symbolism, possibilities and most importantly, ways out of a blocked situation. These are presented to our conscious mind via the unconscious.

The intuitive levels

Many people who find their natural intuitive senses developing start to worry that their insight will be seen as something peculiar and unaccepted. This is part of the earlier stages of realizing the senses. The intuitive process, I've found, is actually divided into two levels or stages:

Stage 1: the basics of psychic development

This stage is seen as the start of a fascination with the unseen: the experiences of feeling someone is there; seeing things out of the corner of your eye; even developing a keen interest in the healing arts. With this stage there's also a fear of your energy being depleted. Some describe this to me as a fear of 'psychic attack' – a term they've heard bandied around as a kind of code to expect others to drain you of your energy resources.

There's a fear of dark forces, an urgency to be able to read people and their lives. People in stage 1 ask me, 'When will I be psychic?' There's an urgency to have an end result, to feel as though their extra-sensory perceptions have some value.

Ultimately what someone at stage 1 wants is to gain an understanding of life at the level of the emotional field, especially if life has become overwhelming for them. They're finding it a tussle between their more surface senses and a fleeting perception of something deeper or predictive. When people access this layer they often want more of it quickly or reject it completely – thinking it's a terrifying indicator they're losing their mind.

Neuroscience researcher Dick Swab says: 'It's sometimes hard to draw a line between spiritual experiences and pathological symptoms. The former can get out of hand, leading to mental illness.' I would tend to agree with this at stage 1 of the intuitive process of development. If this stage is left unmanaged and is mixed with fear and a lack of mind management, and if there are repeating episodes of extreme instances of intuitive insight or psychic experiences, then indeed the question of mental illness does come up.

It's something people who find their intuitive ability suddenly opening up worry about. The general rule is: if you're questioning it, it's a healthy questioning. The fact you're questioning it means it comes from a normal place of curiosity, a desire for balance. Rushing to be intuitive and psychic is not the answer – it comes through in its own healthy time. The less rushed, the stronger the foundation.

I therefore work with the belief that your intuitive progress is a journey, not a destination. There isn't an 'I'm here' notice to hang. It's first and foremost about your access to a deeper understanding of yourself. Your sensory skills are encouraging that access and foreknowledge of situations.

Stage 1 is a necessary part of the development process, but in the initial stages it's propelled by fear. I can't remember my own specific fear at the time of realizing my extra sensory perceptions were opening, but I do remember having a generally fearful nature. There was a growing fascination for understanding why I often knew what was going on in a person's life without asking, but I wasn't frightened of it as such – I was more frightened of the world at large.

> Often, if a person remains at stage 1 of the intuitive process, they have an interest purely in proving something. They need to show themselves, and at times other people, that their intuitive impulses are not part of a vivid imagination.

The problem at this level though, is if the monkey mind isn't in hand, the fear components make the apparent 'psychic' senses more pronounced.

For example, I've seen teenagers with heightened, hormone-driven senses and a fearful imagination start to unconsciously move things. During times of stress, parental divorce for instance, keys have seemingly turned in locks or items have flown from the shelves. These experiences are often thought to be driven by supernatural forces, when in fact they are a powerful expression of a held-in emotion. The feeling is held in by the teenager in order to avoid upsetting a parent. In my experience this only happens to intuitive teenagers.

Stage 2: deepening the intuitive self

This stage incorporates several different distinctions around intuitive thought and impulses. Stage 2 is a choice – it doesn't just happen – and it takes conscious participation. Stage 1 happens to all of those with a Highly Intuitive nature, while stage 2 excels in those who actively participate.

At stage 2 the integration of the 'soul' and 'personality' – now at its height – begins to combine to a level of *knowing*, a moving beyond the limitations of the ego (see chapter 9). With stage 2, at a physical level there's a training of the mind taking place, a conscious interaction that helps to reduce the chaos, fear and tension of the everyday self. It's at this stage we consciously take care of our psychology with our sensory skills, realizing that one doesn't become integrated without the participation of the other. At this point I firmly believe it's vital we start to combine rather than separate.

We live in a society of participation – the realities of our world are that we're part of a combination, and we cannot remove ourselves from the unkindness of the world. We have to realize that it does exist and then consciously evolve our own awareness so we can cope with the processing of it rather than continue to ignore it. As Sensitive souls, we feel the pain of an event deeply; we wince at bad stories in the news, we cringe for people when they are embarrassed, or should be embarrassed, and we cry for the lost child after a natural disaster.

This level of empathy makes us human – it makes something inside of us switch on rather than switch off when we see or hear of an injustice. It makes us part of the whole, rather than sticking us on a mountain-top removed from life below. The truth is, as a Highly Sensitive Person, you're never going to lose it; it's part of you, a sense capability you don't want, much of the time. You can, however, embrace it and use it to your highest ability.

This level of intuitive understanding is also known as 'empathic accuracy', which is broken into four areas:

~ The first is 'the ability of the perceiver in terms of their accuracy in judging other people's personality traits'.[1] In terms of psychic development this is the beginning component. The other person doesn't have to be present; in fact, I find it much easier to look at this when the person isn't in the room because their presence is distracting. It's easier to be more accurate when they are absent.

~ The second area is an 'accurate perception or understanding of each other's attitudes, values and self-perceptions'.[2] I see this as looking out through the eyes of another person: seeing and feeling their world as your own and then accurately feeding the information back. It isn't a view from the outside of the person – it's a very different feeling, as though you are wearing the glasses of their life.

∽ The third criteria 'focuses on perceivers' accuracy or "affective sensitivity" in inferring the emotional state(s) of one or more target persons.'[3] When I'm presenting at an event or online and I'm asked to look into the world of more than one person at a time, I find this information is presented in the psyche through images, feelings, perceptions and information drawn from data I suspect is stored as part of my brain. This is why Intuitive-Sensitives are so drawn to accumulating information, reading books and have a curiosity for as much as they can get their hands on to learn. It's so they can build this part of their intuitive, empathic viewpoint.

∽ Finally, the fourth area 'focuses on perceivers' empathic accuracy – i.e., their ability to accurately infer the specific content of another's thoughts and feelings'.[4]

To date, I'm still fascinated by the fourth part: the view of another's thoughts and feelings are often a surprise to me. The detail in this area depends largely on the liveliness of the target; if they are a gentle person, you receive the information gently, and if they are a nervous person, you receive the nervy feelings. If they are muddled, you receive a muddled feeling before it becomes straightened out for interpretation. Often you can also see or perceive things the target's psyche is already prepared for, but has no conscious knowledge of.

One recent example of this is a person who asked me briefly through an email about a job interview they were to have in a few days' time. I mentioned in passing that I saw them in my mind on a very nice-looking boat. They didn't know at the time that the job interview was to take place onboard a spectacular yacht.

When moving into stage 2 of the intuitive process, we begin to integrate the intuitive self into the rest of who we are, and into society. Stage 1 can leave us a little dreamy and separated from the real world. The process of developing our intuitive nature already started through not only our intuitive impulses, but our empathic nature in stage 1. Stage 2 takes us to the next level of awareness.

It takes time to become who we already are: it's not an overnight job, but the deeper parts of stage 1 motivate us to consciously participate in the journey. Stage 2 of the intuitive process helps us with the motivation to accept the realization of who we are.

Mastering stage 2 intuition

Self-mastery is the active training of the mind. This not only increases our intuitive output, it makes it a very stable sensory skill. At stage 2 of the intuitive process we're no longer plagued by the possibility that our intuitive impulses are vague and unreliable. This isn't brought on by arrogance, rather it's simply the observation of energy as it's present. Our own perceptions, limitations and fears no longer stand in the way of truth.

Most of us in the West think outwardly; we're impacted by what we see as the external reality. We judge our world, our importance in it, by what we're able to prove in the world of other people. Our feelings are dictated by it, our inner peace is reliant on it. Spending our nights worrying about how we're seen in the outer world, trying to minimize embarrassment or doing things to impress others is normal to the human experience.

The issue is, though, that intuitive thought isn't an outward process. It isn't logical or rational and it builds up over a period of time. When you try to measure it, the energy dissipates, moves away in an elusive, unpredictable manner. It's often as though intuition has its own separate consciousness, an intelligence of its own forces.

Active and passive thinking

When aiming for understanding of the super-intuitive state of stage 2, we can look at the human mind as an instrument, one that can be used in two directions. In the outward sensory experience it's a reflection of our contact with the physical and mental world, plus our emotions. With this mix the mind records our sensations and reactions via the five senses. This is both active and passive thinking: active thinking is an act of the will, while passive thinking is an occurrence.

The key is to be able to switch in the two directions, both outwardly (the five senses) when necessary, and immediately inwardly for focus (mind-mastery). Sensitives can train themselves to think both outwardly and inwardly, and it's the inward direction that leads to the super-intuitive state.

Outward thinking distracts us from a direct focus on the intuitive process. Often you see people who were on fire with their intuitive progress in stage 1 start to drift in their perceptions because they haven't refined them through conscious effort into stage 2. This means their inner world became distracted by the glamour of knowing how to see into things in life.

The person started to take this for granted; they didn't work on their own inner world, their psychology, to bring their intuitive senses into line with the humble, connected self. They began to create the separation – the ego nature of the 'personality' being the belief that they are the 'chosen one' or 'gifted'. When this happens, their ability to see truth is lost or underdeveloped. The person can only see then through their own ego rather than the collective whole. This will leave gaps in their empathic nature as the reasoning becomes connected to self-importance and status, an outward focus.

I believe, therefore, that the Intuitive-Sensitive is often 'given' a tough emotional start or experience, not as a punishment or karmic lesson, but in order to remind them of what a wound feels like. This is to help them develop their empathic capabilities, while reducing the impact of the human being's self-centred nature. It builds in the opposite direction of increasing connectivity. When we've enough connectivity within ourselves we can then connect with another. To put it plainly: you're not too soft. Be proud that you cry at the drop of a hat. I am!

Meditation, meditation, meditation

In the way that an estate agent says 'location, location, location' when it comes to buying and selling houses, I say 'meditation, meditation, meditation' if you want to prepare your system for stage 2 of your intuitive progress and consciously participate. In short, meditation helps to train the mind to switch directions and move inwards for its idea of self, rather than focus on the external world. This doesn't mean you sit on the top of a hill for five years chanting 'Om'. Meditation has a variety of formats that work for busy people and enable the mind to re-direct inwardly to allow stage 2 intuitive perceptions.

For Intuitive-Sensitives meditation is a step beyond mindfulness. Mindfulness is the concentration or focus upon a single thing, and this is fantastic for beginning to train a busy mind, as it helps a person to choose what they think, manage negative thoughts and solve a situation from a calm rather than an emotionally heated position. Mindfulness, originally a Buddhist practice, is now heavily used within psychology to alleviate a variety of conditions and to handle emotions.

For an Intuitive-Sensitive, mindfulness is preparation for meditation. In fact, the naturally intuitive person was mindful for much of their childhood; daydreaming and switching focus to a single, simple thing is akin to mindfulness.

Meditation, however, is slightly different and this is definitely the case when you are engaging in stage 2 towards the super-intuitive state. Meditation has an enormous impact on how we manage both our sensitivity and our intuitive nature. It's this active control of the mind as the default setting, rather than a fear-based reality, that helps lead you to a position of deep intuition, one that's achieved through the internal communication between instinct, intellect and intuition.

Next we'll look at how instinct, intellect and intuition relate to the Intuitive-Sensitive and meditation, but first it's important to recognize what meditation is, and how it impacts your intuitive senses. When we're building the intuitive muscle, meditation is more than a quiet contemplation: it's an internal exploration through imagery, sensations, euphoria, release, emotions and healing. The purpose of this is to access the ability to know ourselves.

Within this framework it's possible to settle your sensitivity and open the senses to a richer experience while feeling a deep sense of calmness, even if there's a storm of chaos around you. This enables you to access a more insightful approach, not only to problem-solving, but to the very satisfying ability to help another without having to fix it for them or feel like a failure if you can't.

The best form of meditation for the Intuitive-Sensitive is a guided process, because these help us to more actively access the symbolism of our unconscious thought patterns and history. Given that intuition develops the more we remove what's in the way rather than what we put in there, a guided process will trigger the exploration.

It also helps us to interpret the symbolism we receive from the psyche of other people. The ability to interpret symbolism helps enormously with an Intuitive-Sensitive's confidence because they can quickly realize what's their energy and what's someone else's communication.

Instinct intuition

Instinct intuition is an awareness we have that's very primal in nature. I would describe it as a 'mother's intuition' – a protective energetic instinct that has no boundaries. There are plenty of examples of the protective instinct kicking in: being in the right place at the right time for your child or a close relative would be one. This type of intuition isn't developed or learned.

I believe a woman's intuition becomes heightened or more noticeable during pregnancy, for instance. This may be because at this time a woman is more naturally vigilant and protective. Plenty of women have reported to me that their first awareness of a strong intuitive impulse was during those nine months.

Dr Shamas, a psychologist at the University of Arizona found that 70 of the 100 mothers involved in the 1998 *Intuition in Pregnancy Study* correctly predicted their baby's sex based on gut feeling alone. For many that instinct continues and builds into a wider sphere, but essentially instinct intuition is very much about a primal protection, based on a universal instinct.

Intellect intuition

Intellect intuition closely relates to stage 1 of the intuitive development process. Intellect is the basis of the external world and we use it as a point of reference. This stage of intuitive development allows a bridge of awareness to form between our external perceptions of reality and our internal world. Intellect intuition helps us unite our rational and intuitive thoughts – it's the conscious communication between mind and body.

When looking at the energy of people at this stage of their intuitive progress I frequently end up referring to it as a kind of separation between their mind and body. Often this will be the body, for instance, trying to communicate a hurt in life while the head is trying to suppress it. When someone is at this stage it's easy to feel or even see, a miscommunication between their words and feelings.

If I question it, the person will initially disagree, often quite heavily, until I ask them to 'feel'. It's then that the body makes its message clear, and the head space steps aside to allow the 'body' to release the held energy. A moment of feeling uncomfortable will often disperse the feeling and preoccupation with what was previously bothering the person.

Intellect intuition is obvious – it's certainly not subtle and often is the point at which a person begins to realize they have something going on that others don't. For some it's psychic experiences such as dreaming of events before they happen, having an experience of seeing or sensing someone after they have died, or a feeling about contact from a long-lost friend only to see they've sent you an email when you turn on your computer. This is usually repeated episodes spread out over a period of time before the person takes the hint from within themselves and begins to actively explore it.

Towards the realm of the super-intuitive

This form of intuition is beyond the stages of instinct and intellect, but it's necessary to pass through an understanding of the two in order to really know and feel you want to make the effort for the super-intuitive state.

In the beginning the super-intuitive state is elusive, sporadic and difficult to repeat. This is because it's an ongoing process, rather than a euphoric destination. Neurologically, this energy is closely linked with mindfulness from a Buddhist viewpoint: in this instance mindfulness is the active development of virtue.

In Buddhism, virtue is the rule of 'to do no harm', as well as making choices that extend our emotional and intellectual strengths, build our confidence and our ability to enhance our help to others without losing ourselves.

How the development of virtue works in the brain is as a top-down view from the pre-frontal cortex (front part of the brain) and bottom-up calming from the parasympathetic nervous system, mixed with the positive emotions originating in the limbic system.[5] This means the front part of our brain, metaphorically the view of the third eye in the centre of the forehead, works with the part of the nervous system that calms us down.

To visualize this, imagine a stream of light beaming from your third eye down your body, to meet another beam coming up from the base chakra (base of the spine) to join at the solar plexus (above your belly button).

This combination working together warns the intuitive system of fear reactions that never reach the limbic system (the bit of our nervous system that hits the roof when we're frightened). That means whenever we feel afraid, nervous or overwhelmed as an Intuitive-Sensitive, our system completely and instantly calms down.

The working of it this way around means it's usually the calming of the nervous system for the Intuitive-Sensitive. The focus is to draw up from the base energy and down from the third eye to meet in the solar plexus. In Reiki, the work is from the top chakras such as the crown and third eye. This suggests it's the mind that has to settle first the enlisting of the pre-frontal part of the brain.

With intuitive development, it's the connections we have with the body that need better care. Usually for an Intuitive-Sensitive the third eye (the pre-frontal) is already in fine working order. It's the body that needs to be better understood. This is about feelings, knowing what we feel rather than trying to numb out what's uncomfortable.

This begins the journey to our intuitive wisdom: an awareness that's really an applied common sense where we come to understand what hurts and what really helps to relieve that hurt, knowing it's not an external substance in the form of a food, drug, action or another human being.

I've seen, in the development groups I've taught for many years, how people seem to release a need to continue disruptive behaviours directed towards themselves, especially addictions or habits bordering on them, when they really start to participate at a level of accessing their super-intuitive state. The reason is that they not only allow themselves to see the illuminations of truth, which this part within the self reveals, but also open the door to equanimity.

Equanimity – fulfilling the search for peace

In Latin the word equanimity means the joining of the mind and the soul. It's a state of balance and composure that's completely undisturbed by external events. It's the ability to remain present in your world but not upset by it.

It involves a place within yourself where there's neither apathy nor indifference – you're engaged in the world but not troubled by it. It means a permanent state of balance, a feeling of space around experiences – a space that's wide enough to see.

Evolution has designed us, through the fight or flight response, to react to pleasant and unpleasant feelings. Equanimity is the trained state within the self, remaining balanced at all levels so we no longer experience the extremes of emotion. Highs and lows become a single level of evenness.

> My experience of this energy is by no means perfect, but I do have a level of evenness I've fought for, been through hell for, but would never swap in a million years. In the depths of this adjustment I felt as though my insides had been turned inside out and shaken like an old carpet.

Aiming towards equanimity is the building of faith in seeing life aspects as transient, an imperfection in the nature of experience. From that view, the only view is truth.

I may well have cheated in getting there, I don't know. Many years ago my sympathetic nervous system was cauterized during an operation to correct a fault in it. This certainly didn't impact my levels of sensitivity but perhaps – I'm not sure – it calmed my nervous system reactions. Whether this did impact it or not is anyone's guess, but what I do know is that it didn't stop my system from being shaken again some years later.

In aiming for equanimity, the super-intuitive state is natural to the person getting there. This is because our inner world is no longer governed by fear: the soul and the personality are united in unconditional love, a forever-partner inside, where aloneness feels a distant memory.

Catching the bus to equanimity

In Buddhism there are four pairs of polarities called the Eight Worldly Winds. One takes you the way you wish to go, the other moves in the opposite direction. One attracts us, while the other repels us. These four pairs of polarities are pleasure and pain; praise and blame; gain and loss; fame and ill repute. Equanimity is the development of ourselves where the wind has less impact on the mind; we accept the wind direction as part of our learning and our experience – and happiness becomes unconditional.

We can only accept this if we're prepared to allow a connection to what has been painful, what has hurt us. The transcendence of pain doesn't mean avoiding it. We cannot reach a state of balance if we've never experienced imbalance. We don't recognize light until we've seen darkness.

So how do we catch the bus to equanimity – to access the level of the super-intuitive state within ourselves? We have to accept life as the polarity. It doesn't mean we become fatalistic, always expecting a fall if something pleasant happens. It means not hanging on to something as if it were the only one left. The true power of letting go means we accept that the feeling of pain is a necessary cycle, a part of the polarities of life. Avoiding pain creates more pain, while passing through it means the wind will change.

Recently I was speaking to a woman who was grieving the loss of a relationship; the man had left her some months earlier. This man had not only been her lover, but also her business partner. He'd told her some months before leaving that the relationship was not what he wanted to be in, and six months later, when his decision to leave the business also came to light, she was devastated by the loss.

The man had become involved with someone else – a woman who worked for the company. When I spoke to this lady she was desperate for him to come back; caught in a desire for pleasure, she was prepared to sacrifice whatever was asked, just to be released from the pain. She accepted blame for the breakdown of the relationship, and projected praise onto 'a wonderful man, a life partner'.

Caught in the cycle, this woman couldn't see that her way out of pain was simple. If she allowed herself to see her own light, she'd notice this man's way of removing himself from the relationship wasn't wonderful, it wasn't respectful and it wasn't the behaviour of a life partner. Even if he returned, he'd do the exact same thing again, yet she was prepared to exchange her pain for a moment of pleasure.

Letting herself access her pain – letting the flow of this windy time in her life breeze through her, to feel it close to her skin – would mean it would only last a short time. The wind would pass. Instead, I can guarantee that this woman's avoidance of her pain will steer her boat straight towards choppy waters for a very long time.

Allowing ourselves to access the truth, to see what is presented before us for what it is, not what we would like it to be, leads us to the still, yet fast waters of our super-intuitive state.

Summary and action ideas

∽ The super-intuitive state is divided into two areas. Stage 1 happens to all those with a Highly Intuitive nature while stage 2 is a chosen path. Stage 1 is the fascination with the unseen and it leads to an understanding of the emotional world. Stage 2 requires empathic accuracy.

∽ Active and passive thinking are the key to the super-intuitive state. The trick is to gain the ability to switch in two directions. Outwardly (the five senses) and immediately inwardly for focus (mind-mastery). The ability to switch instantly between the two is the super-intuitive state.

∽ Preparing for stage 2, the super-intuitive state, requires meditation. Equanimity, the joining of mind and soul, is the outcome of stage 2. Equanimity is a trained rather than a natural state.

Chapter 12

Step 6: Courage – the Road to Self-Realization

'It takes courage to grow up and become who you really are.'
E. E. Cummings

A room full of expectant faces, the odd excited tremble, shuffling chairs, a settling down before someone always asks: 'What are you going to do to us this time, Heidi? Will we need tissues?'

During the growth stages, the inner world of the Intuitive-Sensitive feels turned upside down, to the point where we become afraid of our own growth. We're afraid of two energies: success and failure.

The thing an Intuitive-Sensitive wants most is a feeling of freedom, usually from the containment of their own fears. The issue is though, that they sometimes reject what it takes to make the last push to get there. To make the push for growth you have to enter 'courage consciousness'. This is an essential part of the journey; if we try to bypass it, our development can only be limited. Courage is stepping into fear, looking it in the eye and smiling.

What is courage consciousness?

Courage consciousness is the transient energy between leaving the old world and entering the new. When we leave something behind in life, we often feel a sense of sentimental loss, even if what we're leaving had little value in our lives. This is a deep-set issue, programmed into our inner world and overseen by the monkey mind as part of what marks our territory, our domain.

I see that very clearly whenever I try to clear out my children's toy box or a drawer. I have to do it very quietly because it's amazing how kids become very attached to dried-out Play-Doh and broken pencils.

When we enter courage consciousness the old world is the leaving behind of low self-worth, non-productive relationships, approval-seeking and a general lack of personal care, whether that's in the way we look after ourselves or the way we talk to the inner world. The old world is about looking to the external world to fulfil inner happiness; it's essentially the rejection of the soul reality, due to the fears of the personality.

The personality, the everyday self, likes to keep things familiar, the same, no matter what. It may say it wants something to be different, but push it and it will revert back to what it knows. For instance, restaurants, especially fast-food outlets, know people will order the same familiar items and rarely trying something new. That's why new things are always on special offer – it's to try to entice us away from the old favourites.

The new world
Put most simply, the new world is about personal care and love for the self, which creates highly productive relationships, a natural happiness that no longer requires external stimuli, self-approval and a feeling of embracing the 'soul' reality.

The suspended, transient state of courage consciousness can feel static. Intuitive-Sensitives in this space say to me: 'Nothing's happening; I feel blocked, stuck.' In truth, though, *everything* is happening.

You know you've entered this stage in your progression when you feel lost, yet sense a positive outcome, a waiting feeling that isn't the result of procrastination. It feels as though you're about to go through some form of transformation, but without any idea of what it relates to. The reality is that when you feel life has changed so much on the inside, you wonder what the outside will bring.

The journey to courage consciousness

Courage consciousness is more associated with the body than the mind in this instance. We all know how we should do some things and not others. In our head we find reasons why we should do something and the reasons why not to. When everything is focused in the 'head' it's easy to become distracted and separated.

> The journey to courage consciousness is easier to step into if we look at it from the viewpoint of our energy vibration – the idea that we have layers of frequency unrelated to the physical body. Whether someone believes in energy vibration or not is unimportant – what matters is that it's a helpful way of seeing how things connect.

We have several components: the radiant energy body (which can also be referred to as the soul body) and the vital or etheric energy body (which is seen as the vehicle for the life force – our way of connecting to what's unseen, but of which we are aware). The body of 'dark light' is the hidden light of the physical body, and it's through the vital body that all energies flow.

For instance, the vital (etheric) body is said to be fed by sunlight, and it's easily impacted by the radio chatter and static of other people's energy. When it's depleted, the body feels empty and exhausted. Stress depletes it, as well as long-held emotions. As the vital energy is a meeting point for the physical and non-material world, it sometimes carries a heavy burden.

Courage consciousness is the process of the radiant energy body/soul body meeting with the 'dark light' of the physical body. Its meeting point is the vital energy field. This is why many people can trace back a feeling of an awakening process when their body disappeared into Chronic Fatigue. The fatigue gave them a link to something else, a deeper feeling. When the 'dark light' is engaged, it starts the process of enlightenment.

The embracing of the soul light, blending with the vital body, stimulates the physical vibration to its own higher frequency. When this happens, it has no choice but to release any vibration that doesn't match.

This is the reason why Intuitive-Sensitives feel they have gone through a spiritual or opening process. The 'soul' and the 'personality' have connected, and recognized each other. The journey then begins for these two parts of the self to live in harmony. This is the point at which we take the choice to enter our own courage consciousness.

The long, dark night

Any hesitation we have about entering courage consciousness is often knocked on the head by a 'long, dark night of the soul'. These feel like transformation without choice; the personality feels booted into some kind of change. This doesn't usually happen unless we've built enough faith in our own light. The faith in our own light isn't a learned experience; it's something that happens.

My own experience in the area of the dark night has been multiple. Today I can honestly say that there isn't an awful lot left for me to be afraid of. Each experience has taught me something deeper, something more helpful to my own life moving forward and to those to whom I offer my musings. If we're not willing to face our own demons, or have not had the experience, how can we understand another person's?

I believe that for some people, the dark night is inexplicably more forceful than it is for others. The spiritual teacher and author Eckhart Tolle's story is one such example. His forcible shove through courage consciousness happened at the age of 29. Very down on life, he had a cataclysmic, terrifying spiritual experience that erased his former identity and left him in a state of deep peace and bliss. For him, life began at that moment.

I see the experience of entering the courage consciousness phase as different for each individual. Some have huge, instantly life-changing experiences, while others learn from a traumatic event. Whatever the transformation, it's what's appropriate for that person to pass through, their own test, not one placed upon them.

What makes an Intuitive-Sensitive unhappy?

If you ask someone what makes them unhappy, they'll usually come up with an example of an irritation triggered by the outside world. Something another person does – 'leaving the lid off the toothpaste', 'belittling me in front of the children'. Whatever the answer, it will be something touching on the truth, but often it's not the whole truth. It takes courage to admit what really makes us unhappy. It's not always easy to bring to the surface, but it's a necessary evil for access to our deeper understanding.

> It's often difficult for an Intuitive–Sensitive Person to say what makes them unhappy – they feel a strong responsibility to make others happy and therefore seek to solve their woes without making a connection to their own.

When we reach though the stage of courage consciousness, we're faced with no option but to face what makes us unhappy. A pressure builds to release unproductive situations and relationships – what is compromised in our life.

The foundations of these energies are often in reality, rooted in our foremost experiences. Some of these are tough to admit to our inner world, and it takes the building of courage to see the truth, although it's revealed as we deepen the inner relationship and our intuitive thoughts grow.

Why is this? We have to move beyond the basics of stage 1 in our intuitive cycle; if we only see through the perspective of emotions – of others as well as our own – we can only interpret through the changeable experience of the 'astral' focus. The astral focus is the psychic part of ourselves that interprets emotion in the moment. Like all emotion, the astral focus is changeable and reacts to mood, emotions and wishful thinking.

We're all capable of gaining some kind of access to the astral focus. We're experiencing the astral focus when we know someone is in a bad mood and they've said nothing. We see it when we have a feeling that we know who is calling before we go to pick up the phone. We also see it when we have a good or bad feeling about something and later learn we were right.

The astral focus is really a reliance on hopes and desires as an interpretation, rather than what is always actual. That means we remain only able to see through the eyes of avoiding what's uncomfortable, beholden to what we see as social acceptance, what people think and how we're not good enough.

Viewing our world through these eyes, trying to keep the wolf at bay, is what makes us unhappy. Courage consciousness is thus the entry point to giving up the pressure of keeping the wolf from the door. When I was finally tired of it, I let the door go loose, neutral as to whether the wolf ate me. It was at this point that the realization struck me: in releasing the door, and no longer fighting, the wolf was only fuelled by the fear. It wandered in, took a look, and wandered back out again. I haven't been wedged up behind the door ever since.

Blocks to courage consciousness – the 'hated child'

When I talk about courage consciousness to some people their hearts sink, and they slink off in their mind to a hidden cave, right at the back of who they are. They go there to be alone, for it is in there they can nurse the wound of never being 'good enough'.

These particular Intuitive-Sensitives have a strong part of them, deep inside, that doesn't feel worthy of entering courage consciousness; their intuitive senses feel they have reached their limits and they're not meant to take it any further. But why does this hit as their reality? What's wrong? It's because their core basis, the energetic belief imprisoned in their unconscious, is that of the 'hated child'.

The 'hated child' characteristic[1] is an extreme terminology and one that makes most of us wince, but it's an important one to address for the Intuitive-Sensitive, especially in relation to courage consciousness.

Does this mean a person was literally hated? For some yes, the truth is they were; for others the development of this characteristic is somewhat subtle. When a couple have a surprise, a pregnancy they were not expecting or prepared for, depending on their own history, they present the view that this new being isn't welcome. They're not connected to it and they resent its existence.

'Many parents who think they want children find out differently when the full impact of the totally dependent human being is thrust upon them, when circumstances change, or when their resources to deal with the reality of an infant are much less than expected.'[2]

The reason for having a child is for some people a way of connecting with an already damaged romantic relationship; it's a case of not so much wanting a child, but something almost duty bound to love them, to be a reflection of their own idealized self. They want a 'perfect baby'[3] – a compliant, fantasized soul – instead of a defiant little human with their own way of doing things.

Inevitably at some stage the child will 'disappoint this ideal, and the parental rejection and rage which that elicits can be shocking. In every case, it is the real, spontaneous *life* in the child that provokes the parental rejection and hatred.'[4] I believe some of this behaviour in the parent(s) is triggered by the incorrect belief that babies and children have no conscious knowledge of events, that somehow things don't impact them because they don't recall or remember them.

Family stories about babies being left to scream at the bottom of the garden, or force-fed due to milk intolerance or left on a potty on top of a cabinet, only to fall off and bump their head, are normal topics of sentimental laughter in some households.

Therapeutic experiences with clients who share this type of history suggest that, sooner or later, they make two core feeling decisions: (1) 'There's something wrong with me,' and (2) 'I've no right to exist.' The individual has taken the environmental response personally and has incorporated it into her self-concept.[5]

I've seen that the backgrounds of many (not all) Intuitive-Sensitives have evidently had this form of neglect. This then becomes a hugely tricky area for them to negotiate when it comes to courage consciousness. If the parental figure(s) haven't felt that their child lived up to their expectations, how on earth is that child going to feel it can possibly live up to any expectation, without considerable help to see its own light?

Numerous Intuitive-Sensitives report distinct memories of some form of maternal or paternal neglect. Whether this was an acceptable form of social behaviour at the time, it is certainly a leftover of the 'Victorian' view that children should be disciplined with corporal punishment and seen but not heard. For the process of courage consciousness, this default setting of being somehow hideously bad, unworthy and with no right to existence, impedes progress.

If a person recognizes the presence of 'hated child' energy, the worst thing they can do is try to squash it or ignore how it feels. Doing that brings progress to an abrupt halt, as the unconscious switches its setting to 'numb'.

When someone is in this place, they can neither think nor feel. Their intuitive senses become a survival mechanism, making it hard to switch and take the step over to stage 2 development, which in part, is the releasing of the 'hated child'. The best thing they can do is to gently nurture – treat this energy with kindness.

> In adulthood, the hated child character will shut off relationships, testing them to the point of rejection, and they will exercise a level of control so they don't have to become too emotionally intimate. They'll choose partners who are either emotionally unavailable or overly needy, unless they have consciously worked on themselves.

Alternatively, they will turn away from relationships altogether, placing their worth into work, to forget the belief that they don't have the right to exist.

'These people… are keeping the archaic feelings of terror and rage at bay by maintaining a close watch on any circumstances that might trigger these emotions.'[6] With this very colourful mix of emotions, or lack of them, numbness and dissociated states, it's highly important to recognize and accept some of these emotional facts to move through courage consciousness.

The stumbling block can be that the 'hated child' often has to overcome the idea they need to have perfection, a specialness, in order to be acceptable. They approach their intuitive capabilities as something they *have* to be perfect at; to get to the same level as others they think are better than them, rather than focus on it as their way to heal.

This issue has developed as a result of their early unacceptability or inability to live up to the parental idealization, and therefore their unconscious programming is terror, annihilation or disintegration.[7] To focus on healing this initially brings to the fore this level of fear, that somehow their visibility, their presence in the world, only has the one outcome: extinction.

Intuitive progress gives those with this absence of a healthy early attachment or love the ability to connect with their own faith – a level of realizing some form of unconditional love – giving them the courage to heal. 'Decreasing the perfectionism and need for specialness will usually result in decreasing procrastination and/ or performance anxiety if these are problems.'[8]

This phenomenon of the 'hated child' is too common among Intuitive-Sensitives for it not to be a factor worth addressing. This isn't to say all Intuitive-Sensitives have this challenge, but it's too widespread for me to ignore. When I do see someone with the 'hated child' vibration, it's very satisfying to see them make that leap of faith across to the world of themselves: to realize that indeed, they are no longer responsible for parental happiness and are now free as their own person and entitled to exist.

Much to their dismay though, their healing is never perfect – they'll always have the vigilance, the jumpy feeling someone is about to tell them off, whether they are six or 76. But they have through their intuitive progress developed an internal reassurance that instantly says, 'It's okay – you're acceptable. You can cope in this world, and you're not going to be punished for your existence.'

Honour the heart

One of the key connections between anyone carrying the hated child vibration and feeling worthy of courage consciousness is the opening of the heart centre. In energetic terms, the heart energy is exceptionally important for the mind and body to link effectively.

For Intuitive-Sensitives, there's a period in their development cycle in which the heart energy becomes more active. I've noticed that this heart opening happens in all who choose to develop their intuitive progress beyond the basics. It increases their empathic skills and the ability to link healthily to other people's hearts and minds.

The heart centre will, in many ways, begin its own healing journey without conscious input. I've seen how many Intuitive-Sensitives will find themselves suddenly in tears for no reason, and are then perfectly fine (without any signs of depression).

Or their history starts following them around – old, unresolved issues come up to the surface: they bump into people they haven't seen for years, previous partners knock at their door or they start to feel in their body like they've never done before. It's the beginning of their internal world beginning to heat up, a warmth coming into their experience – the beginnings of a blissful state.

Honouring the heart though, means knowing what's in there: what makes you tick, both good and bad – noticing the shadows, and connecting with them, rather than trying to shove them out of sight to the back of the cupboard. It's about scrabbling about in the muck, looking for ways to tidy it and not being afraid to do so.

The most effective route is to *feel* your way in there, through meditation and guided processes. This helps to train the brain component to realize it can have conscious control over the limbic reactions, opening the capacity for instantly effective reassurance.

Heart awareness

Becoming aware of your heart centre means knowing clearly what's important to you, and this will help you to tell the difference between your intuitive messages and fantasy. This exercise will help you to develop your ability to tell the difference between a hope, a desire and the truth – thus increasing your ability to distinguish between insight and imagination:

1. Allow your mind to go blank; it will feel sleepy if it's trying to avoid 'feeling'.

2. Notice what it's doing, and rather than being the thoughts, observe them. Observe what you're thinking.

3. Move your awareness to the centre of your chest. Your breathing rhythm may change.

4. Feel yourself moving inwards, and imagine if you can a giant spongy pink heart shape.

5. Feel your awareness; move inside it.

6. Sit in here, and feel a lift or a drop in the energy as your mind wanders into your thoughts. Begin to discover through the feelings in here.

7. Pop out in your mind through the spongy heart; feel the difference in energy vibration as you come out, having been inside.

8. Repeat this exercise when you want to know something about yourself or your own feelings when solving a dilemma.

Accelerate your progress into courage consciousness

Although courage consciousness happens upon us when we're ready for it, there are ways to accelerate your progress into the full flow of it: to realize the soul's energy. However, there's still the need to respect all other aspects of your inner world, harmonizing at the same time. Remember, too, that this isn't a race: it's a journey not a destination. There's no pot of gold at the end; there is though a consistently pleasant equilibrium and the possibility of equanimity.

The following steps towards courage consciousness have proved the most effective for the thousands of Intuitive-Sensitives I've worked with, regardless of their country of origin or cultural roots:

Step 1: discipline the body

This step involves balancing the physical body. Without making the most of the physical vehicle of our consciousness, progress into the courage consciousness aspect of our development becomes very limited. With increased efforts of working on our energetic vibration, the body begins to build its own 'light' – a feeling of expansion, wellness and bliss. An abused body cannot hold its light: try putting petrol in a diesel car – it just doesn't work.

This discipline doesn't have to be perfect, but it does have to be a conscious effort that's indicative of your willingness to face your demons, rather than shy away from them. To undertake this step, you need to become more aware of what you do to yourself. Rather than judge it though, simply observe it. How do you behave towards yourself? Do you use food to settle an emotion? Do you sometimes decide not to take on something because you don't feel good enough to complete it? Be more observant of the times you feel fear and try to suppress it.

Step 2: honour the heart centre

Allow yourself to find what's important to you in life. It could be a commitment to find your focus, your sense of contribution, to exercise your empathic generosity in a healthy way, with the promise within the self to overcome your desire for a secured outcome before action. To take action anyway, even if it's small steps.

Do this through reassuring yourself as you would a child when it's frightened. Children often won't do something unless they are encouraged. This happens within our inner world, too: the child-self is often still trying to talk to us. It talks us into backing off doing something important in case we fail; it can't bear to feel the pain of failing. If you reassure yourself when you think you might be feeling this, you'll be surprised how brave you really are with a little encouragement.

Step 3: heal the emotional body

This is the letting go of stored resentments: the freeing of them by consciously making an effort to no longer indulge in self-abusive habits or to hide them. For example, admitting you eat a bar of chocolate every night or drink too many glasses of wine means you are halfway to choosing it, rather than using it. This is the courage to heal anger and identify its source.

Step 4: clarify the mind

This step is adjusting your life's focus into proactive, rather than reactive. This is the transformation that enables you to seek to resolve a matter, rather than just reacting to it; in using your mind, rather than the reaction of the emotions to find solutions to issues. This enables you to start to find your own centre, and gives you the ability to start to control nervous system reactions – you choose your response rather than your nervous system overreacting and triggering fear.

As an Intuitive-Sensitive you will find that many of these steps are already in motion for you. I've found by the time someone is interested in what I have to say, they have made a lot of their own inner progress, whether they realize that consciously or not. The way to see it, is to look back on your life. You'll find that the way you respond to events now, compared to how you reacted to them five years ago, is considerably different.

You'll find that you now have better internal resources for dealing with the events, situations and things that frighten you. You may not have understood how you got there, but you do find that things bother you for a shorter period of time. The reason for this is that you have already developed a decent level of control over your own mind. You have a stronger sense of self-awareness and have already made the conscious decision to heal what doesn't work as your balance in life.

Don't be ashamed of your kind nature

Many Intuitive-Sensitives are ashamed of their kind nature – they believe it's a softness that lets them down. Sensitives consistently ask me how they can toughen up. I don't have the answer to that: and for me, it's not about toughening up – in fact, it's the opposite. I find strength comes in vulnerability. A hard lesson to learn, but one that I've experienced time and time again, as the expression of a truth.

Vulnerability doesn't mean 'victim', though: far from it; victim suggests something that's defenceless, incapable of protecting itself. Intuitive-Sensitives are far from being victims – they are the first to jump in to defend someone who cannot defend themselves. They have 'have-a-go hero' hard-wired into their system.

I've heard countless stories of amazing heroism in Intuitive-Sensitives. Many though, have been taken advantage of, their inner world bruised by the fact that less scrupulous people have used their nature for their own ends. I've heard how their kindness has been used and abused by others who don't have their integrity or conscience.

I've also seen how many Intuitive-Sensitives have left work they enjoyed because they felt their levels of integrity let them down in an organization more focused on a quick outcome than treating people well. The compromise they were asked to make was too much for their system to bear. It collapsed under the strain, the body became ill and they left with stress-related illnesses they often then spent years trying to correct.

Others continue in working environments they feel are slowly killing them because they don't operate with the same conscience they do. They try to solve it every day, feeling that what's obvious to them as a solution falls on deaf ears. All of these issues are desperately frustrating to the Intuitive-Sensitive. Yet it isn't always their job to fix it, even though they feel it should be. These are the worries that wake them in the early hours in a cold sweat.

The key is to begin to have the courage to realize you don't have to take on the frustrations of other people, even though you think it's your job to fix them. The courage to not take them on comes from honouring how we actually feel rather than trying to numb our own pain by taking on someone else's. The courage to feel our own feelings comes from practising self-nurture. This isn't how many cakes we do or do not eat or how much chocolate we consume, it's taking a moment to notice when the person inside ourselves is distressed.

Summary and action ideas

∿ Courage consciousness is the transient energy between leaving the old and entering the new. It is necessary for self-realization.

∿ The 'hated child' is the residual energy held in a person's psyche due to their belief that they have not fulfilled an expectation. The 'hated child' of the Intuitive-Sensitive is released by opening the heart centre energy.

∿ Self-realization is accepting that vulnerability is a strength, not a weakness.

Chapter 13

Step 7: Unite the Inner Child and the Adult

*'My quest these days is to find my long lost inner
child, but I'm afraid if I do, I'll end up with food
in my hair and way too in love with the cats.'*
KENNY LOGGINS

Hurrying along, opening doors, closing them, feeling a rising panic pounding through her heart, Sophie searched desperately in this never-ending corridor of doors. Eventually, she opened the right one and ventured into the dark room. She approached the trap door with trepidation and her world slowed down as she descended the creaking, musty stairs into the cellar below. She had a sense of foreboding and a fear pounding in her gut, and she could feel her body temperature rapidly changing. There in front of her, dressed in rags, stood the lost child.

A life lesson from the child in rags

There comes a time within our spiritual and personal growth when we feel an overwhelming need to connect with the authentic self. When our relationships feel less worth it unless they are filled with mutual respect, when our work becomes lifeless without purpose and we're no longer interested in keeping up with the Joneses, we know the authentic self is coming to town.

Trouble is it has a silent aggressor looking to keep it at bay. The aggressor is distant but there. Its presence is known but unknown; its influence powerful, creating havoc yet never seen. It reacts badly to criticism; it attracts impulsivity and drama; it likes constant stimulation. It's both attention-seeking and rejecting. It demands constant attention although you've rarely, if ever, seen it.

Sophie saw hers. It or rather she, was dressed in rags down in the cellar. About seven years old, she stood silently staring with flaming eyes, yet was helpless. She had something to say, yet was too emotional to say it. Finally, someone, the most important someone, had come to find her because she cared enough to look for her. Relieved, she collapsed into her rescuer's arms and said, 'Am I free? Can I come out now?'

We all have an inner child and an adult self. When the inner child and adult self are separated from each other, a void exists within the self. The child feels abandoned and the adult cannot find its lost child. The two selves wander helplessly; they're searching for each other in an isolated wilderness or looking in a mass of other lost children.

Inside, this feels like an 'aloneness' – a feeling of being misunderstood, the body looking for attention. The adult self overworks to hide its pain of searching but not finding; anxiety rises and there's a drive to work harder. And so the story continues.

As the intuitive self develops, it provides a contact between these two parts of the self. The adult occasionally hears the child calling; the child feels that somewhere the 'parent' is waiting. This gives the child hope; it searches further as it 'knows' the parent will find it. These two parts of the self translate as the child (personality) and adult (soul) – see chapter 7.

When these two parts of the self find each other they unite, merging into a unified soul energy, a realization of what is known in Eastern philosophy as the causal body. When the child self is damaged, it has no healthy reference: no concept of where it belongs. A feeling that the 'parent' self is somewhere out there gives it the inclination to keep going. The intuitive self sends the signal the parent is waiting, and the causal body tells us it is found.

The causal body is known as the highest subtle energy body housing the true soul. It is responsible for the highest creative aspect and the deepest part of the soul essence, where our true inner self manifests. Our wisdom is stored here. The causal body originates from yogic concepts – for this analogy I've adjusted it to the theosophical interpretations of the Buddhi-Manas.

When it comes to the child self and its healing, from what I've seen, this part of the self doesn't respond well to logical process; it prefers stories, dreams, a feeling of fantasy in order to connect. Its connection though to the 'parent', the soul, is a driving force it cannot ignore.

Many Intuitive-Sensitives refer to this awakened desire to find what they are looking for. They discover that the world of attaining things for the sake of it feels hollow to them. When they tap into the energy of their inner wisdom, the feeling that the two worlds of the personality and soul have collided, they have reached an energetic frequency high enough to release their deep world of internalized, unconditional love. For this to happen, it's the journey of how the inner child, the inner adult and the causal body join in a peaceful union.

Self-separation

Many Intuitive-Sensitives are very self-sufficient, good at providing comfortable scenarios for other people but limited in providing that opportunity for themselves. This self-separation creates what author John Bradshaw describes as the 'split self'. At this point you see yourself as an object rather than a feeling person, separated, as if you're no longer in the 'me'.

I see many people in this scenario during the early stages of their intuitive development; it's as though they are elongated, as the stretched part of themselves isn't in the body, it's floating somewhere above them. When in this position the person will feel vacant, not really in their body and certainly removed from their feeling world.

As the experience of life then becomes absent, there's a feeling of emptiness and exposure; the question 'Who am I?' begins for many an interest in self-development. This is the time when I often hear a Sensitive complain that they feel overwhelmed by the feelings of others – they no longer feel strong enough to fend off invaders.

The feeling, as Bradshaw says, is 'they are after me, and they are going to take me by surprise. The hunter is always approaching. There's never a moment I can relax. I must be constantly guarded lest I'm ever unguarded. I'm alone in the most complete way.'[1] The child self will therefore often create a long-lasting, almost unbreakable loyalty and commitment to things that aren't good for them.

Love as the great connector

For soul and personality to connect, love must be present. The soul already expresses love as the parent self. It's whole shows the inner child (personality) unconditional love, but the child will not accept it, trust it, without first feeling loved. The preceding steps are all to help the personality develop confidence – an ability to establish and trust its decisions.

As it does, it relaxes its defences to let the parent self of the soul in. To do that effectively, the personality has to understand its capacity for instant inner nurturing. This nurturing calms the monkey brain's automatic reactions; it stops us searching outwardly for the parent self, which in turn creates a deeper experience of happiness.

Whether we like it or not, we humans are shaped to parent, to love. Sat above our ancient and simplistic brain mechanisms is the relatively newly evolved cortex, which has an enormous influence over the rest of the brain. This part is shaped by our evolutionary pressure to survive through parenting, bonding, communication and love.[2]

In today's society, as our industrial needs reduce and technological requirements increase, I believe the intuitive, almost mind-reading parts of our brains are under pressure to expand. As society has got faster, we need to access information at ever increasing speeds.

The expansive component of right-hemisphere thinking allows us to accept this increasing speed. If, though, we're continually burdened by the weight of containment, the safety of what's known through the generations, it significantly slows the process. This results in a lot of frightened people. Their reptilian brain, scared for its survival, will struggle to keep pace with its evolved twin.

As Eric Schmidt and Jared Cohen observe in their book *The New Digital Age*: 'In the future, computers and humans will increasingly split duties according to what each does well. We will use human intelligence for judgement, intuition, nuance and uniquely human interactions; we will use computing power for infinite memory, infinitely fast processing and actions limited by human biology.'

This advancement in the way things will work in the future is another reason why our internal world needs to be more united. With the inner child and adult self working together in harmony, Intuitive-Sensitives will be far better equipped to accept the deeper skill of intuition as part of our working life rather than seeing it as an indulgence we try to keep away from the world.

Who is the ranker in your life?

As we focus on creating the loved child and the happy inner adult through the connections of the causal body, it's helpful also to realize the effectiveness of understanding linking and ranking. As Highly Sensitive People we're more impacted by feedback, and therefore we learn easily from our mistakes.[3]

Although we learn quickly from them, making mistakes means we're apprehensive when it comes to the possibility of repeating errors. We'll hold back when we'd learn more by pushing forwards. To help the child and adult self unite for the personality and soul realization to happen, one of the quickest routes is to increase our ability to observe rather than absorb uncomfortable emotions. For most Intuitive-Sensitive People that's much easier said than done.

How do we improve our ability to absorb less? By understanding linking and ranking. We all have rankers in our life – those who use power to manipulate. As Intuitive-Sensitive individuals we are kind, gentle and compassionate. We have felt unusual and separated from others during our early life, as others have seemed to have a harsher nature than our own. Into our adult years we've hidden at the back, felt unheard, tried to dampen down our sensitivity and disengaged our intuition. We've been terrified of the predator energy – we've felt inside that it's hunted us down – we've worried over what others think, we've had sleepless nights worrying about how we'll be criticized or torn down over our desires and wishes.

Freedom from much of this cycle of an internal nightmare is instantly available through understanding the impact of linking (connection) and ranking (power).[4] Self-ranking creates the feeling of failure determined by the feelings of guilt and shame. Linking, on the other hand, creates acceptance, happiness and ultimately, soul connection, which is much more in line with a sense of purpose.

Our ancestors had a pecking order – the higher you were the more influence you had. A challenger who wanted to rise above the hierarchy would be equal to confrontation. This would result in the winner or the loser. Avoiding mistakes by having an instant unconscious sense of your strength was a level of self-protection.[5]

The questions asked of the self would relate to how much social support, confidence, skill and intelligence we had to rise to this challenge. If the questions didn't amount to a strong enough answer, the internal response would be – *better not fight, save your energy*. This, as our biological defeat response, is equal to depression and shame, making it more likely we'd accept the low rank rather than compete for the higher position.[6]

That response happens to us today when our Sensitive system has to avoid many defeats. Our system has become hyper-sensitive to ranking (power), as too many defeats impact our self-worth. Failure feelings surface and our system is flooded with the emotions of defeat and shame.

> *Ranking is when we rate ourselves against others, or when others rate their importance against us – the idea of 'pulling rank'.*

When a female meets another female for the first time they are aware, either obviously or sub-consciously, of being given the once-over: the glance from head to foot. A male meeting a male for the first time is aware of the overly firm handshake. Both are tools of the power play, ranking.

The Sensitive individual is very astute when it comes to another human and their attempts at social climbing; this means as a Sensitive, you're more likely to rank yourself inappropriately against others. We rank ourselves too much to prevent future defeats and humiliations. We therefore rank even if it's not present from another individual.[7] When you rank yourself inappropriately against others, you establish fewer links.

So, how can we tell if someone is ranking us? People who you feel bad around rank you. You'll feel judged in their company, as though there's an all-out competition about who is the better person. You'll notice that conversation switches to ways in which one is trying to out-do the other. It's rife at the school gates, in corporate interactions and at dinner parties. It's an unfortunate component of the basics of human nature.

Using linking to defeat criticism

In contrast, the people you feel good around, link. They are the people who contribute to us feeling comfortable and accepted. While ranking makes us unhappy and anxious about our worth, linking makes us feel accepted, connected and happy.[8]

Linking, however, is all about the Sensitive. In today's society we're not like our ancestors – survival is now about teamwork, connection and character. It isn't about power plays and competitions for climbing to the top of the tree. Life is speeding up, and there isn't the time for all that now, even if we wanted to.

> To be skilled at linking we have to allow ourselves to be liked, understood and helped. We don't allow this because of the old problems of self-rank. When we switch to linking, the fear of failure disappears into the background. Why? Because we then feel connected, not judged.

An inadequate balance between the internal rank and linking mechanism creates criticism, ridicule and undermining. It's an experience we're all familiar with, whether presented in our outside world in another person or within our inner world of self-rank.

Your first experience of an abuse of power may have been in adulthood. Sometimes, this can be more traumatic than if you first experienced it in childhood. The shock that someone can be so undermining can bring a Sensitive to their knees. Repairing that damage is essential for the inner parent and child development, as this helps to ensure that others have a minimized impact.

But how do we do that? Do we have to spend our life avoiding such interactions in order to remain healthy? No, we don't and it's not realistic to try. Unless we live as a recluse at the top of a hill, never interacting with people, we will inevitably come across a ranker. The way out isn't to avoid, it's to link.

Linking

Linking is the fast route to healing our inner critic and the effects of criticism in our lives. This linking exercise will help you to resolve any built-up resentment that may be holding your intuitive progress in limbo.

1. Allow yourself to feel the inner critic rising; feel it naturally or focus on someone who makes you feel uncomfortable to be around.

2. Allow the feeling to rise in the body – you'll start to feel agitated.

3. If it's a person, then allow them to come up in your mind. See or sense them in front of you. As you begin to feel the emotions of shame, instead of bowing your head, hold it high.

4. Imagine taking the feeling from where it is in your body, pulling it out, in your mind, and showing it kindness. Hold it in your imagination – you are holding the emotion gently. Then put the feeling back inside.

5. Keep repeating these steps – using the person who ranks as the figure in your mind – until your facing them in your mind feels neutral.

6. If faced with ranking in a real-life situation, say the following in your mind: 'It's okay, it's just a ranker.' If you can, offer a link – a neutral handshake or a kind smile.

Activating the causal body

Understanding the essence of the inner-child vibration, and its challenges for us in everyday life, helps us to make significant progress when entering the world of the causal body, the point at which these aspects of the personality and the soul really begin to unite, to form a lasting and unbreakable bond.

As we tap into an energetic frequency high enough to unleash a wealth of stored wisdom, the internal world feels evidently more comfortable with uniting the child- and parent-self. During this process, I've seen how a lot of Intuitive-Sensitive People take an interest in the possibility of past lives. This is as the causal body develops its 'light' – an opening into a deeper component of inner knowledge, a kind of releasing of density from the energetic field.

The causal body is said to be inactive in most people, but I would say it's active in all Intuitive-Sensitives. It's a live energy, pulsating with the 'living fire' of the authentic self. The causal body is said to remain colourless and transparent in those not ready to activate this level of self-awareness.

In its Hindu origins, the causal body is said to be for those who aren't ready to know their awareness of it; it remains a means for the soul to incarnate into the physical world. Its firing into life in the Intuitive-Sensitive would therefore make sense; why would they begin to have an interest – even a fleeting one – in the meaning of possible past incarnations? Do we repeat life or live once? This is a cultural question that's considered the norm in the East but seen as ridiculous in the West.

The belief is, as a person develops the matter of the causal body, the soul's house is stirred into activity with vibrations through the lower energy bodies of the personality. This is why it's necessary for the personality, the child-self, to work through its – for want of a better expression – earthly psychology.

As we learned earlier, without love personality and soul have no relationship. Without this relationship life can only reflect the lower aspects of the personality. Life becomes a constant drama. Initially, some people love the drama – it gives them a feeling of aliveness, a connection to emotion and a sense of importance. In the grand scheme of things, it can only lead to a search for love as an experience in the external world, an expectation that others are there to fulfil our wishes, rather than we are there and responsible for fulfilling our own.

What prevents us from allowing full access to our intuitive state, to the development of the causal body, is our efforts to self-rank. Consistently comparing ourselves to others, deciding we're 'less than', is a very time-consuming exercise. It means we never get anything done, we severely limit our achievements and we procrastinate to the point of pain.

Intuitive-Sensitives have asked me on many occasions if they are 'good enough' to join a particular group or train in a certain area. They are desperately keen to, they want to, but their inner self-rank holds them back from it. This saddens me; I love to see people come to the things I do simply because they want to be there, to give things a go, to enjoy what's on offer for no other reason than their self-development.

This I believe, is the route to the opening and connection of the causal body, as the personality begins to relax, to enjoy itself and commit to its efforts. We can do this through one of two ways: focusing on the 'left-hemisphere' preference for reason and rationality through a focus on brain development – a mindfulness centred on the physical world. Or we may find more benefit in focusing on a non-contained world – the energetic world – one that feels more akin to our 'right-hemisphere' preference of wonderment, expansion and intuition.

I believe that both of these routes ultimately lead to the same conclusion, once active participation is initiated and continued.

Summary and action ideas

~ As the intuitive self develops, it provides a contact between the child-self and the adult-self. The adult occasionally hears the child calling; the child feels that somewhere the 'parent' is waiting. As the intuitive self develops, these two connect.

~ Hindu belief says the causal body is the 'living fire' of the authentic self. As the inner-child and adult-self unite, the causal body expands. For most people the causal body is inactive, but for the Intuitive-Sensitive it is active.

~ Rankers in our life manipulate us. Linkers connect. Understanding these two aspects of ourselves, or how they are in other people, helps to unite the two selves.

~ Love is the connection. Developing it for the self begins to unite the child and adult selves.

Afterword

Among the thousands of Highly Intuitive-Sensitive People I've helped over the years I've seen one very common factor. They begin believing they are weak, unable to get over this overwhelming and uncomfortable feeling that they can see into other people. They experience the world of other people as though it's their own, and the pressure of doing that becoming too much.

What they don't yet believe or see, is what I've seen in many of the people I've worked with: Intuitive-Sensitive People are the toughest, most resourceful, loyal, kind and generous people you'd ever want to meet. They are hidden as the gentle soul, often on the fringe of a gathering, rarely the upfront, in-your-face person, unless they have learned it as a defence mechanism.

When I've introduced non-Sensitives to a room full of Intuitive-Sensitives who are, or are in the process of becoming, more at home with themselves, they stare in wonderment that such a group exists. Intuitive-Sensitives are the people you feel instantly comfortable with – they notice; they take their role seriously but are always unassuming.

If a crisis arises, it's the Intuitive-Sensitive who will be there. They are so used to running from themselves, especially in the initial stages of their intuitive development, when it comes to them being asked to stand-up for someone, for what they believe in, they are there, the first to volunteer, even if they're afraid. They are the have-a-go people: the ones you have to pause to see.

My life's passion

In my years of not only teaching this subject but very much experiencing it, I've noticed that little can rub your sensitivity up the wrong way like it used to once you allow yourself the full flow of your development expression. Is there an end? When do you get there? I don't believe you ever get there, but you know you're going in the right direction when you no longer see it as a destination.

You see it as a continuation of a journey – one with no destination. What I do know is that once you allow the path to unfold inside you, you're never again bored. Boredom seems to leave your world the further you exercise the muscle of the intuitive self. Something replaces it: a kind of gentle excitement in all things, a fascination for what you currently don't understand and an openness of thought.

I'm passionate about Intuitive-Sensitive People because of what I've seen them do. They are life's extraordinary people – hidden among the ordinary. Like most Intuitive-Sensitives, my entry to this world was not a chosen one: the intuitive self came upon me as a road to discovery, thrust upon me as a route to recovery.

In early childhood I was a silent child. I rarely spoke; I was incredibly shy and suffered a multitude of stress-related conditions. Bullied from all corners, criticized 'for my own good', seeing deeper into the meaning of my world became a link to understanding it.

In adult life, through intensive connection and work within the intuitive side of myself, I've developed the ability to utilize my sensitivity to play an extremely useful part in my life. My parent and child united, I've built and maintained a happy life, one with a strong foundation of intuition, something that saved my sanity.

My husband complains he cannot surprise me; my children think I'm spooky; I seem to know when everything is coming. Whether it's subtle cues or I can feel it in the 'ether' I'm annoyingly usually right – it's an instinct beyond a female 'knowing'. This I believe is the impact of the Intuitive-Sensitive: there are millions of us out there, untapped and waiting to find our true selves.

References

Chapter 2: What is an Intuitive-Sensitive Person?

1. Aron E. *The Highly Sensitive Person: How to Thrive When the World Overwhelms You*, London, Element, 1999

2. www.hsperson.com

3. Aron E. *The Highly Sensitive Person: How to Thrive When the World Overwhelms You*, London, Element, 1999

Chapter 3: 'You're Too Sensitive'

1. Felitti V.J., Anda R.F. *The Relationship of Adverse Childhood Experiences to Adult Health, Well-being, Social Function and Healthcare*, Lanius/Vermetten/Pain, Cambridge University Press, 2010

2. Aron E. *The Highly Sensitive Person: How to Thrive When the World Overwhelms You*, London, Element, 1999

3. Gerhardt S. *Why Love Matters: How affection shapes a baby's brain*, Routledge, 2009

4. Tomarken A., Davidson R., Wheeler R. and Doss R. Individual differences in anterior brain asymmetry and fundamental dimensions of emotion (1992), *Journal of Personality and Social Psychology*

5. Swabb D. We Are Our Brains: *From the Womb to Alzheimer's*, London, Allen Lane, 2014

6. www.hsperson.com

7. Schore A. *Affect Regulation and the Repair of the Self*, 2003, New York

Chapter 4: Intuitive-Sensitivity and Right-Brain Thinking

1. www.hsperson.com

2. www.spherion.com, 2013

Chapter 5: Recognizing the Opening Process

1. Peters S. *The Chimp Paradox: The Mind Management Programme for Confidence, Success and Happiness*, London, Vermilion, 2012

Chapter 8: Step 2 – Learn to Manage Your Mind

1. *Psychology Today*, 2014

2. Raichle M.E., MacLeod A.M., Snyder A.Z., Powers W.J., Gusnard D.A. and Shumlan G.L. A default mode of brain function, 2001. Proceedings of the National Academy of Sciences 99:10237-10239

3. Yang E., Zald D., Blake R. *Fearful Expressions Gain Preferential Access to Awareness During Continuous Flash Suppression*, Vanderbilt University, Copyright 2007, The American Psychological Association

4. Jiang, Y., He, S. Cortical Responses to Invisible Faces: Dissociating Subsystems for Facial-Information Processing. (2006) *Current Biology*. 16(20), 2023-9

Chapter 9: Step 3 – Make the Transition from Personality to Soul

1. Swabb D. *We Are Our Brains: From the Womb to Alzheimer's*, London, Allen Lane, 2014

Chapter 10: Step 4 – Cope with Others and their Power Struggles

1. Swabb D. *We Are Our Brains: From the Womb to Alzheimer's*, London, Allen Lane, 2014

2. Pressman and Pressman, 1997

Chapter 11: Step 5 – Access Your Super-Intuitive State

1–4.Ickes W. Empathic Accuracy: University of Texas Arlington (1993) *Journal of Personality*, 2006

5. Hanson R., Mendius R., *Buddha's Brain: The practical neuroscience of happiness, love and wisdom*, Oakland, CA, New Harbinger, 2009

Chapter 12: Step 6 – Courage, the Road to Self-Realization

1–8. Johnson S. Character Styles, London, Norton, 1994

Chapter 13 : Step 7 – Unite the Inner Child and the Adult

1–3. Bradshaw J. Healing the Shame that Binds You: *Health Communications*, 2005

4. Dunbar R., Shultz S. Understanding Primate Brain Evolution, Philos Trans R Soc Lond B Biol Sci. Apr 29, 2007; 362 (1480): 649–658. Published online Feb 13, 2007

5–8. Aron E. *Psychotherapy and the Highly Sensitive Person*, Routledge, 2010

Bibliography

Aron E. *The Highly Sensitive Person: How to Thrive When the World Overwhelms You*, London, Element, 1999

Babiak P., Hare R. *Snakes in Suits: When Psychopaths Go To Work New York*, Harper, 2006

Clance P., Imes S. The Imposter Phenomenon in High-Achieving Women, *Psychology: Theory, Research and Practice*, Vol 15 (3), 1978

Dunbar R., Shultz S. *Understanding Primate Brain Evolution*, Philos Trans R Soc Lond B Biol Sci. Apr 29, 2007; 362 (1480): 649–658. Published online Feb 13, 2007

Felitti V.J., Anda R.F. *The Relationship of Adverse Childhood Experiences to Adult Health, Well-being, Social Function and Healthcare*, Lanius/Vermetten/Pain, Cambridge University Press, 2010

Gerhardt S. *Why Love Matters: How affection shapes a baby's brain*, Routledge, 2009

Goleman D. *Emotional Intelligence: Why it can matter more than IQ*, London, Bloomsbury, 1996

Hanson R., Mendius R., *Buddha's Brain: The practical neuroscience of happiness, love and wisdom*, Oakland, CA, New Harbinger, 2009

Ickes W. Empathic Accuracy University of Texas Arlington (1993) *Journal of Personality*, 2006

Jiang, Y., He, S. Cortical Responses to Invisible Faces: Dissociating Subsystems for Facial-Information Processing. (2006) *Current Biology*. 16(20), 2023–9

Johnson S. *Character Styles,* London, Norton, 1994

McGilchrist I. *The Master and his Emissary: The Divided Brain and the Making of the Western World*, London, Yale University Press, 2009

Peters S. *The Chimp Paradox: The Mind Management Programme for Confidence, Success and Happiness*, London, Vermilion, 2012

Pink D. *A Whole New Mind: Why Right-Brainers Will Rule the Future*, London, Marshall Cavendish, 2008

Ross-Kubler E. *On Death & Dying: What the Dying Have to Teach Doctors, Nurses, Clergy and their Own Families*, London, Routledge, 40th-anniversary edition, 2008

Schmidt E., Cohen J. *The New Digital Age Reshaping the Future of People, Nations and Business*, London, John Murray, 2013

Schore A. *Affect Dysregulation and Disorders of the Self*, New York, Norton 2003

Schore A. *Affect Regulation and the Origin of the Self*, Hillsdale, NJ: Lawrence Erlbaum Associates Inc, 1994

Schore A. *Effects of Secure Attachment Relationship on Right-Brain Development, Affect Regulation and Infant Mental Health*. Department of Psychiatry and Behavioural Sciences, University of California

Shamas V., Dawson A. *The Intuition in Pregnancy Study*, University of Arizona, 1998

Stout M. *The Sociopath Next Door*, New York, Broadway Books, 2005

Swabb D. *We Are Our Brains: From the Womb to Alzheimer's*, London, Allen Lane 2014

Tomarken A., Davidson R., Wheeler R., Doss R. Individual differences in anterior brain asymmetry and fundamental dimensions of emotion (1992) *Journal of Personality and Social Psychology*

Weaver I.C.G., Cervoni N., Champagne F.A., D'Alessio A.C., Sharma S. Epigenetic programming by maternal behaviour (2004) *Nature Neuroscience* 7 (8), 847–854

Yang E., Zald D., Blake R. Fearful Expressions Gain Preferential Access to Awareness During Continuous Flash Suppression, Vanderbilt University, 2007, The American Psychological Association

Acknowledgements

Thank you to my clients and loyal 'members' – without their stories, lives and healing, this book would not have been possible.

Thank you to Anne, Stephanie and Allison, who read, laughed and cried over the chapters, giving me valuable feedback during the writing of this book.

Thank you to Hay House and Carolyn Thorne, who freely gave her time to help me define what I wanted to articulate in the beginning. Thanks to Debra, for a great edit and voice for the final manuscript.

A special thank you to my amazing friends and helpers Catherine, Allison, Stephanie, Anne, Claire, Saima and Caroline, who make what I do possible. Thank you to Jon, who kept my husband sane during the writing of this book. A special thanks to Hayley, whose late nights and patience are second to none.

A deep gratitude for my husband and children: I owe my life to their love.

ABOUT THE AUTHOR

Philip Nash

Heidi Sawyer is known worldwide for her work with intuition and the human mind. As an author, speaker and online trainer she helps people heal their connection to self-love through intuitive development at workshops, online courses and her supportive membership Circle.

Heidi lives in Surrey, UK, with her husband and two sons.

www.heidisawyer.com